POLISHING UP THE BRASS

POLISHING UP THE BRASS

Honest Observations on Modern Military Life

Michele McCormick

Stackpole Books

Published by
STACKPOLE BOOKS
Cameron and Kelker Streets
P.O. Box 1831
Harrisburg, PA 17105

Printed in the United States of America

10 9 8 7 6 5 4 3 2 1

Library of Congress Cataloging-in-Publication Data

McCormick, Michele, 1950–
    Polishing up the brass: honest observations on modern military
    life / Michele McCormick.
              p.   cm.
    ISBN 0-8117-2257-0
    1. United States.   Army—Military life.   2. McCormick, Michele,
1950–   . I. Title.
U766.M34   1988
355.1'0973—dc19   87-16021

To Don

Contents

Parts of this book have appeared in substantially similar form in the publications and on the dates indicated:

"Moving," *Army Times*, November 8, 1982; "Be Prepared," *Army Times*, July 15, 1985; "No Phone," *Army Times*, December 20, 1982; "The Shoes," *Life in the Times*, June 16, 1986; "Gold-Plated Bases," *Army Times*, May 20, 1985; "Speaking Mississippi," *Army Times*, October 21, 1985; "Homesick," *Army Times*, November 22, 1982; "Shamming," *Army Times*, June 7, 1982; "On Line," *Stars and Stripes*, October 9, 1981; "The Uniform Code," *Army Times*, November 18, 1985; "Milspeak," *Stars and Stripes*, August 28, 1981; "Mind over Matter," *Army Times*, January 14, 1985; "Specializing," *Army Times*, September 2, 1985; "Paying Up," *Army Times*, April 8, 1985; "The Colonel's Wife," *Army Times*, May 2, 1983; "Article 15," *Stars and Stripes*, February 12, 1982; "A Fan," *Army Times*, August 23, 1982; "Command Desire," *Army Times*, September 5, 1983; "Oh, Poop," *Army Times*, May 7, 1984; "The Meetin' and Greetin' Colonel," *Stars and Stripes*, July 17, 1981; "We Wives Are People, Too," *Life in the Times*, April 14, 1986; "The Bare Facts," *Stars and Stripes*, July 8, 1981; "Rendezvous in Russia," *Stars and Stripes*, February 21, 1982; "The Mail," *Stars and Stripes*, June 26, 1981; "Driving in Naples," *Army Times*, November 15, 1982; "Armed," *Army Times*, January 17, 1985; "Imagining Life without Dortmunder," *Army Times*, May 17, 1982; "Effective Phrases," *Army Times*, November 11, 1985; "Choosing Career Fields," *Army Times*, June 10, 1985; "To Get Ahead, Be Important," *Army Times*, February 27, 1984; "While the General Sits on the List," *Army Times*, February 11, 1985; "Paranoia with Good Reason," *Army Times*, October 7, 1985; "Wimpy Joe Is Your New CO," *Army Times*, January 9, 1984; "On Not Making the Cut," *Life in the Times*, March 3, 1986; "A Hero," *Army Times*, May 13, 1985; "A Helper," *Life in the Times*, March 10, 1986; "A Mother-To-Be," *Stars and Stripes*, September 1, 1981; "Michele," *Army Times*, October 28, 1985; "Mary Ellen," *Life in the Times*, November 24, 1986; "The First Sergeant," *Stars and Stripes*, January 17, 1982; "An Army Bride," *Army Times*, May 24, 1982; "Name Dropping," *Army Times*, April 23, 1984; "Smokeless," *Life in the Times*, July 7, 1986; "Missouri Punch," *Life in the Times*, June 30, 1986; "Greensleeves," *Army Times*, September 24, 1984; "The Form," *Stars and Stripes*, March 30, 1982; "An Instructive Offer," *Army Times*, June 24, 1985; "Exceptional Ability," *Army Times*, July 19, 1982; "How Assignments Are Made," *Army Times*, August 29, 1983; "A General Drag," *Army Times*, September 20, 1982; "The Main Man at JCS," *Army Times*, August 19, 1985; "General Housing," *Life in the Times*, September 29, 1986; "Ten Tips to Stardom," *Army Times*, February 28, 1983; "General Entertaining," *Army Times*, October 15, 1984; "Bruce," *Life in the Times*, September 15, 1986; "Choir Robes and Combat Boots," *Army Times*, October 25, 1982; "Captain Lorence," *Life in the Times*, April 28, 1986; "Independence Day," *Stars and Stripes*, July 4, 1981; "Living Insecurely," *Army Times*, October 11, 1982; "Giving," *Army Times*, December 5, 1983; "Memorial Day," *Army Times*, May 30, 1983; "Wall of Names," *Life in the Times*, May 26, 1986; "A Handy Guide to the Hierarchy," *Army Times*, October 29, 1984; "Call It Otis," *Life in the Times*, January 6, 1986; "Equal Ashtrays for All," *Army Times*, July 22, 1985; "Military Soap," *Army Times*, January 17, 1983; "Dare to Be Bare," *Army Times*, June 13, 1985; "Mailish Myths," *Army Times*, May 27, 1985; "Year of Values," *Life in the Times*, December 29, 1986; "Guidance," *Life in the Times*, October 6, 1986.

Acknowledgments

My thanks to Mert Proctor, Managing Editor of the European edition of the *Stars and Stripes*. It was Mert who first agreed my thoughts were worth sharing with a military audience and who passed along many invaluable insights about the business of being a columnist. *Army Times* editor Lee Ewing made a similar decision not long after, and his support and encouragement were much appreciated. At *Life in the Times*, Donna Peterson and Barry Robinson have provided me with professional guidance, honest feedback, and that commodity so valued by the worker in the field — an ongoing source of moral support.

The column from which the selections in this book were taken would not be possible without the contributions of those of you who live the military life. You have shared your stories and your viewpoints; your letters and comments ensure that I don't lapse into lazy or hazy thinking. For taking the time to read and to respond and for offering up a wealth of material of broad interest, I thank you all.

A special note of gratitude to my husband. He's never seen my columns before they were printed; he's never worried about how their contents might affect his career. He is a willing resident fact-checker, my most exacting critic and biggest booster rolled into one. He is, in short, living proof that the military does attract the best.

Finally, my regards to Denny McAuliffe, a pal from the old high-school days I ran into unexpectedly one evening in the *Stars and Stripes* Press Club. It was he who first proposed that I should try my hand at writing a column about day-to-day military life. Thank you, Denny.

It turned out to be a good idea.

Beginner's Glossary

The military world has its own particular language. For those of you unfamiliar with these forms of expression, here are some of the terms you will encounter in the following pages.

ALERT. An exercise that involves getting up very early in the morning and reporting to duty as would happen in an emergency such as war. Some people show up for these, some people don't. Some people know about them in advance, some people don't. The best part about alerts is the wonderful names the exercises are given. Names like Laramie Ladder and Running Renegade and Wild Hare. Alerts are not popular.

APO. Army post office. A military-operated mail system that delivers mail to bases all over the world at U.S. postage rates. Sometimes the mail even reaches those to whom it was addressed.

ARTICLE 15. A form of punishment used to discipline soldiers who've been naughty, but not wicked. An Article 15 can mean being busted, fined, or confined to quarters, but you don't go to jail.

BDU. Battle dress uniform. A camouflage uniform that replaced the green Army fatigues a few years ago. In the beginning they shrank. That's been fixed, but they're still uncomfortably hot in the summer and cold in the winter, and it's hard to roll up the sleeves with the camouflage on the outside. Also, they have a lot of oddly shaped pockets and are almost impossible to iron. Looks like they're here to stay.

CO. Commanding officer. The most important person in every soldier's life.

DINING FACILITY. Used to be called mess halls, but the Army has more class these days.

E-NOTHING. A recruit, the most junior of the junior, so low he hasn't earned even one stripe. Usually a pretty nice guy.

FPO. Fleet post office. Same as the APO, but run by the Navy.

IG. The inspector general. Not usually a general at all, the IG is the person who sniffs out waste, fraud, and abuse and considers the merits of soldiers' complaints on a wide variety of matters. Most military units are busiest when they're preparing for the IG to show up and inspect. The best way to pass an IG is for the CO to prepare a lengthy descriptive briefing on successful unit missions and give any real goofballs the day off.

MOS. Military occupational specialty. These are jobs, such as clerk (71-lima) or rifleman (11-bravo) or whatever. Your MOS has a direct bearing on the likelihood of getting promoted. The greater opportunities your MOS training will provide when you return to civilian life, the less likely it is to get you promoted in the military.

MP. Military police. In the Air Force, AP, for air police. In Navy circles, SP, for shore patrol.

MRE. Meals ready to eat. These plastic packets of dehydrated material described as "food" replaced C-rations a while back. You need fresh water to fix some of the main courses, and, of course, you can't heat a packet as you can a can. Some soldiers don't try to rehydrate these preparations. They taste equally bad, dry or wet.

OER. Officer efficiency report. Performance rating on your current job. It's a pass-fail system—either you max the report, or you're down the tubes.

PCS. Permanent change of station. You'd think we'd just say "moving," but we don't. Maybe just because we've learned to love to talk in acronyms.

POV. Privately owned vehicle. My car. Your car. Not the government's car.

PT. Physical training. This is what soldiers do to stay in shape. If it's basketball teams or wrestling matches it can be fun. If it's jogging four miles in formation three times a week it's not.

REAL WORLD. For soldiers stationed overseas, it's the United States of America.

SQT. Skills qualification test. A system of testing soldiers to see if they know what they are doing. About as popular as alerts.

TDY. Temporary duty. It could be a day or a year, but it's still considered temporary, as opposed to a PCS, which is permanent. When it's temporary, the government doesn't have to move your furniture.

Introduction

Polishing up the brass—in the military it's just one among dozens of necessary skills the civilian world simply doesn't appreciate.

Military life is different.

When you're in the military, either on active duty or as a family member or (cursed official term!) *dependent,* you don't live quite like the rest of American society.

Military people move a lot. We get so we can't imagine what it would be like to be in one place for a long time, and—to some of us—the very idea becomes almost frightening. I know people who start to get the moving itch after eighteen months or so. Long before they have the slightest idea what the next assignment will be, the urge to start packing becomes almost irrepressible.

Military people are more likely to mark the passage of time by their moves than by the years. When people ask me how long I've had my dog, I always say "Since Germany." If they want to know when that was, they'll have to stop and wait while I figure it out. It was before Italy and after Pennsylvania. Sometime in the early eighties, then.

Even if you don't know a person is in the military, you can tell the minute you step inside the door of their home. For one thing, the furniture never fits. There's either too much or not enough. And the stuff is from all over—bargain brass from Korea, some Hawaiian teak, a nice display of Italian ceramic dishes, a cluster of *Volksmarching* medals, an early American bedstead bought at auction in the Midwest, and the marvelous grandfather clock that was inherited and has miraculously survived every move . . . so far.

Military people develop an amazing talent for taking an assigned living space, often a cramped apartment or plain little duplex, and turning it into something uniquely individual. All the travels and the moves add up to a life filled with rich experiences. Walk into a military family's home and that richness shows.

Even so, not all the experiences are upbeat. There's no such thing as a soldier who doesn't feel the system has worked him over a time or two, a wife who's never wept when informed of the next assignment, or a child who looks forward to every new school with glee.

But there's a wonderful thing about military people: We understand each other. We help each other over the rough spots.

Military people are friendly. They are always interested in knowing new people, because the old ones are continually moving away. You get so you keep in touch with the people you really care about, and the others you just remember fondly.

The longer you're in the military, the more people you'll run into again and again. It's a funny thing about seeing the same people in different places—a person you didn't like at all at Leavenworth may be a wonderful friend at Fort Dix. Or vice versa. Some people are just nicer and more interesting in certain places than others. I don't know why this is. As far as I can tell, the Pentagon has never done a study on it.

Military people are also accustomed to adversity. For one thing, the Bad Guys are always on our minds. If there weren't any Bad Guys, we wouldn't need a military, now would we?

Then there are the people who work on the post. Most of them are nice and helpful. But there are a few who seem determined to thwart your most basic needs. Like the lady who assigns housing. Or the guy who gives out quartermaster furniture. Or whoever takes job applications at the Civilian Personnel Office.

Whatever service you need most—that office is where the crankiest person works. It's a fact of military life. Somehow, we all learn to get things done anyway.

Despite all we have in common, we military people are sometimes guilty of misunderstanding each other. Nobody in the military is rich, but no matter what rank you are, it sure seems like the people just a grade or two higher are living a mighty posh life.

And nobody in the military is all-powerful—basically, we all work for the politicians—but occasionally a person gets a slightly bigger office and decides that makes it okay to try and rule the world. Or at least the building.

There is also a certain amount of interservice rivalry. The Navy life is toughest, but takes pride in the strongest traditions. The Air Force is the most modern service, but its members don't know how to rough it. The Army has the largest, most complex bureaucracy, but is still willing to try new ideas.

We all have our own viewpoints.

There are three ways to get into the military family. You sign up, you marry up, or you're born in. I took the second route. I had no idea what I was doing.

I was a typical civilian, and the ignorance of most civilians is amazing. I knew about corporals, because I'd seen them in key roles in various World War II movies, and I knew about generals, because I'd met one once at a cocktail party.

Otherwise, I had all the usual misconceptions: I imagined top-quality merchandise would be practically free at the PX. I thought colonels lived in palaces and single soldiers occupied modern Holiday Inn-style rooms. I believed uniforms really could be washed and worn and I was certain my husband would be put in charge.

The reality was just a little different.

In the end, though, I came to like reality better. The reality is being part of a caring community wherever I may happen to live and being around people who are involved in work that matters in a big way.

The idea for a column about day-to-day military life was suggested to me by a former high-school chum in 1980. I'd been living in Germany for a year, working in a military travel office, when I ran into a friend I hadn't seen in years. He was an editor on the staff at the European edition of the *Stars and Stripes*. When I told him I'd been doing some freelance writing, he suggested I submit a column to *Stripes*. I did, and some months later the column began to appear on a twice-weekly basis. A year after that it moved to *Army Times*, and in January 1986, it became part of *Life in the Times*, a section appearing in each issue of *Army, Navy*, and *Air Force Times*.

This book includes a selection of pieces spanning the years since the column first appeared. Time has changed my perspective on a few of the stories. In this post-Nicholas Daniloff era, my conversation and gift exchange with Alex, the Russian soldier (chapter 4), seems foolish. But at the time I was every bit as interested in talking with Alex as he was with me, and the viewpoint he provided was fascinating. Still, given the same opportunity today I'd probably decline.

And the controversy over the rolling of BDU sleeves mentioned in chapter 7 has been resolved: All sleeves must be rolled up with the camouflage out. This means we'll need an extra twenty minutes if war is ever announced. That's about how long it takes to execute this complicated maneuver.

Outsiders see the military bureaucracy as a huge, unchanging monolith. It isn't like that at all. It's changing constantly. The flow of amendments to existing regulations is a river in its own right. Sometimes it seems as if changes in promotion and pay policies are announced daily. They're timed so that when a soldier meets all the qualifications for the next grade—new requirements are added. And periodically there are announcements that most of the current uniform will either soon be obsolete or else it will not. Keeping up with the changes is one of the great challenges of military life. Finding someone who knows how things currently stand is another.

Along the way I've learned the main rule of survival: Laugh or go bonkers. And I've learned another thing too, something I believe more and more Americans are coming to recognize. That is, our military personnel and their families are doing the job right.

From the beginning my purpose in writing the column has been twofold: to amuse you with the slightly skewed perspective that is my way of seeing things and to pass along some of the many insights you have offered me. In the military we have much in common, but we sometimes live in worlds apart. There are many wives who've never heard of "getting over," and at least as many soldiers who've never attended a coffee or tea. As I see it, the more we know about each other, the more harmonious our lives will be.

If you are part of the military family, you'll find friends and familiar situations on the following pages. If there are no uniforms in your life, here's a chance to see the military in a slightly different way: from the inside out.

I hope this book will make you laugh, make you think, and take you back to places you would like to remember. I hope it does many things for you, but there are certain things you can only do for yourselves.

When it comes to polishing up the brass, you're on your own.

1

Moving and Mayhem

The Thrill of New Places

Moving

In case anybody is wondering what my favorite part of military life is, I'll be glad to tell you. I like moving. I like moving, and everything associated with it, so much that it's hard to decide what my favorite part is.

I like the fact that I never have to worry about get-down-to-it spring cleaning. By the time my house cries out for that kind of attention, it's surely time to move. Or almost time, anyway.

I like getting ready for a move.

It's so much fun to look around the house and try to decide what to keep and what to throw away and what to cart up to the thrift shop. If you've led a military life for a while, you find that those decisions don't come easy. Not that the house is full of wonderful things—on the contrary, most of our wonderful things turned up broken or missing two or three moves ago. It's just that it's hard to part with the stuff that's survived. My name-tag collection, for instance, or the set of purple tumblers I once won as a door prize.

But military life teaches you not to become attached to material goods. It forces you to keep your life's accumulation within a pre-determined weight limit.

I like that.

I like it when the movers come.

I believe that movers are not bad people. I believe that most of them really care about our things.

I like getting to know the movers. They can tell, too, and so they hardly ever pack the crystal and the lamps together. They don't toss boxes around in front of me, and they don't ask a lot of questions about our stereo system. They leave me with the feeling that one day I really will see all my belongings again.

I like a challenge. I don't mind driving down a highway with the car so overloaded there's no possibility of seeing out the rear window. I don't become discouraged when we arrive at the new place, suitcases full of winter clothes, to find the climate mildly tropical. Such minor setbacks are all part of the fun.

It's always exciting to arrive at a new place. First, you get to see if the MPs will let you through the gate. If it's a high-security place, you may be required to have a special pass. Those are issued at an office just inside the gate. But you can't get in the gate until you get the pass.

You see why it's such an experience?

Then there's the thrill of house hunting. Anything suitable is generally twice your quarters allowance. So you stay in a hotel, you're a person of leisure. And you and your spouse and the kids and the dog get to enjoy real family togetherness.

I like it when we finally find a place to live and our household goods show up. I like the tingle of suspense: What will be water damaged? What will be missing? How will we get the king-size bed up these tiny stairs?

Moving in is like Christmas. It also teaches you the value of small things. The freezer shelves, the piece of metal that holds the bedframe together, the dishwasher connection. Lose these, as we always do, and you rearrange your priorities.

So, if you were to ask me what I like the best about military life, I'd tell you right away: I like moving. But I couldn't say what it is about moving that I like best.

It's all so much fun.

Be Prepared

You say you're moving? Big deal. Everybody's moving.

All the same, you have to watch out. You have to be careful so you don't let yourself in for the big D. That's disappointment. Maybe even depression. We're talking general downer here.

The problem is, the place you're going to is likely to make a bad first impression. That's what you have to brace yourself for. When you first get there, when you get off the plane or drive up in your car, there are going to be some immediate impressions, some first-day incidents. They are going to be bad.

This is nothing to get worried about. It's nothing to be upset over. You just have to prepare yourself so you can carry on, and be alert in case any good things do happen after a while.

But at first, when you first get there, watch out. Watch out for these things.

1. *The people.* The people in the new place do not look right. They are dressed funny. They are acting strangely. They are either cold to you as a newcomer or suspiciously friendly. They have either hordes of screaming, misbehaving children or no children at all. They are all either trim Linda Evans/John Travolta clones, or else the countryside is populated by blimpos. Either way, you don't like it. These people seem unnatural. After being around for one day you haven't seen a single person you'd like to get to know. They are all too weird. You begin to worry that after three years you may fit right in.

2. *The base.* The base was clearly built for people who like mazes. The roads twist around and then don't link up. There are no directional signs at critical intersections, or, if there are, each sign lists fifty million locations, but not the one you're looking for. As far as you can tell, the housing area is at the end of the missile range and you can only get there when they're not firing. The support facilities are only open during your duty hours. You pull up outside your new office to check in and an MP rushes over to make you move—you've parked in the CO's spot. It's not marked, but everybody knows it's his.

3. *The town.* The town is very near or very far away. It is incredibly sleazy, or uncomfortably posh. It is not like the town you just left and to which you had grown somewhat attached. It is not

convenient. It is not attractive. It is not the kind of place where you will be able to feel at ease. This town does not seem to offer any of the advantages of the last town. It is different. Different does not appeal to you.

4. *The weather.* You've been told that the median temperature is 75 degrees. It's only when you arrive that you realize that means some days it's freezing and the rest of the time it's above 100 degrees. It's incredibly hot or cold the day you arrive, and everyone is rushing to get inside to the heating or air-conditioning. The place where you are staying does not have heating or air-conditioning. The wind is blowing a dust storm across the region, and you express the hope that the wind will blow this bad weather away. A local person tells you the wind blows all the time. Except right before a tornado comes.

5. *The job.* The job was better in the last place. Theoretically your own role was similar, but in fact you can see that this job should have been given to someone considerably more junior or more senior than you. You are overqualified or else not ready for this type of work at all. In this place they seem to overenforce the pettiest regulations or else disregard them completely and work under appalling conditions. You wonder why you were sent here.

Stop wondering. Perk up and look on the bright side.

This place is heaven compared to where you're going three years from now.

No Phone

No telephone.

I am in shock.

I knew there would be deprivations when I married into the military life. I expected challenges, inconveniences, hardships. But I never—even after all my years of experience—I never knew how rough life could really be. Not until now.

I am not a sissy. I am not a coddled, spoiled sort of wife. I've been in difficult situations before and I've toughed them out. I've even enjoyed the satisfaction of conquering obstacles and adjusting to new lifestyles. You think maybe I've had it easy? Let me put it like this: It's been six years since I've lived in a house with a garbage disposal, and that one didn't work very well.

Did I complain when we moved to Hawaii? Never a word. You didn't hear me grumbling about cockroaches big enough to saddle and ride. Turn your back on sandwich makings in your Hawaii kitchen and they disappear before you can say boo. In Hawaii the roaches are so huge it takes only two of them to polish off a whole tray of cheesy olive hors d'oeuvres. They are so numerous that a political action committee represents them in the state legislature. But I never groused about them. I just sprayed my house with poison gases every time I went out and stayed mum.

Then there's the time we lived in a little teeny town in Pennsylvania. I had to drive forty miles to find a decent dress shop. There were just two restaurants in town. One featured hot dogs and the other featured hamburgers. That was to discourage competition. The house we lived in was so small I had to go up the stairs sideways, even though I met all current weight standards.

But you didn't hear me talking about the problems. I knew it wouldn't do any good.

Like when we moved to Germany. Day after day I risked my life on the autobahn with nary a whimper. I ignored the possibility of permanent damage to my lips and went ahead and learned to pronounce the essential words like *Fremdenverkehrsburo*. I ate the best of the wursts, and I braved brigades of blisters to finish weekend *Volksmarches*.

Along the way there have been particular moments when I thought I had truly plumbed the depths. I thought it was grim in Germany because I only saw the sun for two days each year.

I thought it was grim in Hawaii, because I'm allergic to everything that grows there.

I thought Texas was tough, because it was so hard to get the sand out of my nose.

But I got through those hard times because there were other things to make up for the difficulties. Like usually I had a washer, a dryer, a stove, a stereo and . . . a telephone.

Now I live in Italy and I have no telephone and no hope of getting one.

The bright side is, with the money we save on telephone bills, we can build our own private Taj Mahal when we return to the

States. The other bright side is, nobody can tell us about alerts or other unpleasant business.

But the bad news is far worse.

No telephone means no restaurant reservations. It means no calling around to plan an informal get-together. It means no way to cancel your dentist appointment at the last minute. No sharing of gossip tidbits.

Without a telephone I'm spending a lot more time talking to the dog. Life is pretty hard, but I'm going to try and make the best of it.

I wish I could call my mom and tell her what a brave girl I'm being.

The Shoes

You should see my garage. Or maybe I should say, lucky thing you can't see my garage. That's where all the junk is.

A lot of the stuff didn't used to be junk. It used to be good stuff. Like the Berber rug that I stupidly acquired shortly before I got an untrained puppy. The rug was once gorgeous, but now it's ruined. One large corner was destroyed when the dyes ran while I was trying to clean a moderately inconspicuous stain.

Still, I can't bring myself to get rid of it. I'm saving that rug for the day we live in a house with a trapezoidally shaped living room.

Then there are the bar stools. Once, in ancient times, my husband lived in a place with a bar, and these bar stools were an important part of that era. Those days are gone but the memories linger on and so do the stools. They live in the garage, and they seem happy enough there. Every now and then my husband goes out and looks at them, and that seems to make him happy, too.

The garage is also crowded by a color console TV that's too good to throw away and too old to sell. There's a portable dishwashing machine that I'd have to pay to have hauled away. And there are three or four jugs for keeping coffee hot, still new in their boxes — my mother-in-law gives me one every year or so.

Then there are the shoes.

This is a pair of man's shoes that I've been hanging onto until I can figure out their history. The thing about the garage is this: Everything in it has a history. That's important, even if a thing is useless. Every time I look at those coffeepots, I think of my sweet mother-in-law.

The shoes don't have any history. They are a man's black work-shoes, high around the ankle. They have steel toes and look to be about a size 12. I don't know where they came from. I don't know how long I've had them.

The whole thing is borderline embarrassing. One day my husband was cleaning out his closet and he came out with the shoes in his hand. "These aren't mine," he said. Well, I told him, they're definitely not mine either.

We moved to California from Italy. No Italian would wear shoes like these, so we must have gotten them before Italy.

We moved to Italy from Germany. They could be a German workman's shoes, but the only German workmen who ever visited our home were the movers, and, as I recall, they all left with their shoes still on.

In fact, try as I might, I can't think of any time over the past ten years when any person has arrived at my house with shoes on and left with bare feet.

A thing like that would tend to stick in one's mind.

When we realized the shoes weren't ours, we put them in the garage. They've been out there bothering me ever since.

I'm the kind of person who feels good about getting rid of things. A mild clutter is all it takes to keep me happy. I would get rid of the Berber rug, if it weren't almost good enough to keep. And I have divested myself of old suitcases, old clothes, worn-out furniture, and tasteless hostess gifts without a backward glance.

I'm disturbed to find unknown stuff taking up my space and creeping into my weight allowance. Deep down, I'm afraid that maybe these shoes materialized spontaneously among my goods. Maybe there are more things to come. Maybe my garage is in danger of becoming terminally choked with junk that I never got to enjoy back when it was good stuff.

I hope not. I like to think that everything I own once brought me pleasure. It's knowing the happy history, and therefore knowing the good time is over, that makes it easy to throw stuff away.

I'd like to know the history of these shoes. I'd like to know how they found their way to my household and where they were before. Until I can figure that out, I'm keeping them in the garage.

Gold-Plated Bases

A recent newspaper headline really got my attention. The headline said: "Budget for 'Gold-Plated' Bases Draws Fire." The accompanying article was based on a report by a private research group called the Center for Defense Information. According to the Center, the military is wasting millions of dollars on unnecessary luxuries such as libraries, auto hobby shops, and child-care centers.

Well let me tell you, if there's one thing that burns me up, it's talk about "gold-plated" military bases. I'm a taxpayer, too, you know. I'm also a military family member and an upstanding citizen. What I think is that if there are some gold-plated bases around, I should get the chance to live on one. Fair is fair, and I'd like my share.

I've heard talk of gold-plated bases ever since I've been around the military, but I've never actually seen one. Come to think of it, all the stories I've heard have been secondhand. Apparently, during the late 1950s, all the bases in Thailand were gold-plated, which is why so much nice jewelry comes out of there these days. But those are tales that old-timers tell and I'm not that interested in ancient history. I want to know where the gold-plating is today.

Unfortunately, most tales of current gold-platedness are all too easily deflated. I have a friend who lives in Germany in gold-plated quarters. This is a fact. I have seen the manse in person.

Unfortunately, under close scrutiny, the gold-plating has worn thin enough to reveal there's only tin beneath. My friend's huge home is very old, and in the interest of historical preservation it retains the original plumbing and wiring. The resulting inconveniences have nothing to do with my concept of a life of luxury. In addition, my plucky friend has sole responsibility for keeping this three-story white elephant clean. "I can keep up if I do a floor a day," she told me recently. So much for her gold-plated existence.

The problem with the people at the Center for Defense Information is that they don't understand the nature of military life. Auto hobby shops are not gold-plating. They are the places where soldiers go to try and make their cars roadworthy again. Auto hobby shops are essential, because few Germans know how to fix a Chevy Nova, and few soldiers stationed Stateside can afford to pay $200 for a tune-up. A soldier is able to live on a soldier's pay because he can save bucks by using the facilities at the hobby shop.

Libraries are not gold-plating. The library is the place where you go to read reports written by people like the yo-yos at the Center for Defense Information. Then you can look up your congress-man's address and mail off a quick rebuttal.

It's also pretty obvious that anyone who thinks child-care centers are gold-plating has never been a working mother (or single father) and probably has never spent more than two minutes in the com-pany of a child.

Gold-plating is something else altogether. On a gold-plated base there are plenty of quarters for everybody, and you move in right away without having to live in a hotel or transient quarters at all. Cleaning teams spruce the place up for free when you leave, and all yards are maintained by professional garden crews.

All the quarters have built-in dishwashers, every sink is equipped with a garbage disposal, and wall-to-wall carpeting is provided. There is also at least one television station that is broadcast in English and that everyone receives clearly.

Gold-plated means plenty of parking on post, a PX big enough to turn around in, and nice schools on post, or close by. Gold-plating means actual mail and newspaper delivery to the quarters, barracks that were built within the last twenty years, and office buildings that are heated if it's cold and air-conditioned if it's hot.

Somewhere there's a military base with all these features and a few others I haven't space to mention. That base is gold-plated. I've got my ear to the ground for specific news of that idyllic spot, because if I can only find out where it is, I'd like to spend a couple of years there, checking out all the gold-plated details.

Speaking Mississippi

After five years in Europe I was really looking forward to getting back to America, where I could feel at home with the language. But life isn't fair. My plan was to plant myself with my Southern relations while hubby went off to be trained to do something use-ful. And so just as I was recovering from the strain of struggling through survival Italian I was faced with a new challenge. In these parts you've got to speak Mississippi or die.

It isn't the accent that gets me. As a child I often listened to people talking Mississippi, and so I know that the word *thing* has two syllables and the phrase *you all* has only one. That part's easy.

I also am used to the fact that a lot of people have two names. The first day I was here I was introduced to Betty Tharp, and I got a big laugh when I called her husband Mr. Tharp. Because of course she is Betty Tharp Simpson, and he is Tommy Joe Simpson, and what a riot it is to call him Mr. Tharp.

All that is no problem. It's the actual words that mess me up. Take *little*. To me, *little* means small. So you can see how I got confused when people said things like, "I've just rented my house to the cutest little married couple," or "I have a little repairman working on my roof," or "Mary Belle's little boy is teaching economics up at the university." I got the impression that the South was full either of midgets or of child prodigies, and I was most curious to discover which.

Of course, what I discovered was that people were talking Mississippi.

Just when I started to get the hang of *little* I ran into *old*. When people who are speaking Mississippi use the word *old* they're not usually talking about age. And if a sentence combines the words *little* and *old*, you can be absolutely certain that no reference to either age or size is intended. Typical usage might be, "I just bought the finest little old pickup you ever did see." I've learned this means the big new truck is real nice.

I'm beginning to get the gist of speaking Mississippi, and I've learned I have to be careful about my own speech. The phrases I always thought were so clear are not always perfectly understood around here. Say I make what seems a straightforward observation, such as "The weatherman says it's going to be 90 degrees out today." Nine out of ten times the response I get is "You don't mean it!"

Well, I do mean it, and in the early days of my visit I often made the mistake of saying so. Why would I have said it if I didn't mean it? It took me a while to realize that I was creating a problem by speaking in a foreign way.

"I declare," my grandmother would tell me, "I'm going to bake a pie today." And then she would do it. Or "I declare," she'd say firmly, "it's time to mow the lawn again." And I could look out the window and see that she was absolutely right. On the other hand, if a visitor started making departure noises and said "I'll be leaving now," you could bet that person would stay as firmly rooted as Mississippi kudzu. People around here don't do anything or believe anything on the basis of a simple statement. It all has to be declared or else it just doesn't count.

Once I got that figured out people hardly ever said "You don't mean it!" anymore. They knew I meant it, because I declared I did. And when things were serious, I learned, I'd better make sure I said, "I do declare." For instance, I'd be sure and say, "I do declare the kitchen is on fire." Or "I do declare, Annie Jo had a gentleman caller while her husband was away on business."

Another thing about talking Mississippi is that you have to use a lot of superlatives. If you eat lunch at someone's house and then tell them it was really tasty they'll be very disappointed. What you have to do is say that those little old catfish and hush puppies were the very best you ever did eat in all the whole wide world. And to make sure the compliment sticks you can't just say it, you have to be sure and declare it.

If you don't do this, after you leave everyone will say "I wonder where she did learn her manners?" Which is Mississippi talk for saying that you clearly never learned any manners at all.

A few weeks is not long enough to learn to speak Mississippi. It's just long enough to pick up a few basics. I'd kind of like to stay on a while and try to get really fluent. But it's nearly time for me to head along to the new assignment in California.

I do declare I can't wait to see how they talk out there.

Homesick

Somewhere along the line it hit her that she'd lost her sense of home.

It wasn't a rude awakening or a sudden realization or anything like that. It was more like a small, empty space inside her that grew and grew until she had to acknowledge that something was missing. Home was no longer a part of her.

"Where are you from?" was the usual opening question when she'd meet new people, and for a long time she quickly mentioned the name of the town where she had been raised, had gone through her early years of school. But even though she still had friends there, it had been a long time since that town was any part of her or she of it. She hadn't visited it in years; her folks had moved away and made a home in a place that was foreign to her. So after a while, when the inevitable question came up, she found herself mentioning the name of the last post. Hood, she'd say, or Leavenworth or Stuttgart. Some place like that, where she had lived for a while in a military community.

The change wasn't really a conscious decision, it was just something she began to do automatically, because those places held more meaning for her. And so she was surprised one evening when her standard response was met with a chuckle and the follow-up, "Yes, but where are you really from? Where's home?"

That made her pause, because it was a question without an answer. Yet it didn't seem right to tell a stranger that there isn't any home in your life. So she thought it over carefully.

What was home?

Home and her hometown were clearly not the same thing. Go back there and she'd be just another stranger, no different from any other new arrival. That isn't home. Home, she knew, is a warm place, a comfortable place, a place where there is no sense of not belonging.

And home, she knew, is not the town where her parents live, not the town where her husband's parents live. Those are fine places, decent towns, but neither holds anything for her. "Come home for Christmas," her mother had suggested one year, and she'd had to stop and think just where that would be. She has no home in the town where her parents live, though there's no harm if they want to call it that. It only means a moment more to register just what place they are talking of.

"Your house?" she'd asked, to clarify, and her mother had responded with a startled "Yes."

Over the years she's accumulated a mountain of furniture to fill a house she hopes will one day be her home. Where it will be and what it will be like are still mysteries. Travels have made her collection of items an odd mélange. Some things Oriental, others gathered from the various corners of Europe and flea markets and auctions in the Midwest. How it will all go together is hard for her to imagine. There has never been a time when all of it could be assembled together comfortably under one roof. In the back of her mind she supposes that putting those things together under one roof would make it a home.

But home, she knows, is more than a place where your things are. And a good thing too, because for much of her married life her things have been scattered wildly—in storage or on the way or under someone else's care or lost. No, things don't make a home, though she hoped that one day her things might make her home a nice place to be. If she could ever work it out.

And home, she had to admit, isn't even the place where you are living with your family now. "I'm at home wherever I am," one of her carefree friends had announced at a party one evening. "My husband, my children—when we're together we're at home."

Maybe. Plenty of people say they believe that's true. But home, she had come to believe, really has to be an actual place. A house in a town where you'll live for years. A place you take care of and love and put something of yourself into. A place where, even if you do go away for a while, you do it with the knowledge that you will be back and home will still be home.

Home, she remembered reading somewhere, is where the heart is. No doubt that's why the ache of its absence is a pain that never quite fades away.

2

Getting Over

Necessary Skills in Military Life

Shamming

I hear a lot of the troops talking about getting over and shamming, or shamtime. It's plain to me there's some confusion concerning getting over and I thought it might be useful to clear the matter up.

If you're sitting at your desk and you're not doing any work, that is not shamming. You can't say you're shamming just because you've got nothing to do. If somebody were to give you something, you'd do it. If you tell people you're on shamtime, you're indulging in baseless bragging.

But say you're sitting at your desk writing up the specs of the ideal stereo system. The first sergeant comes in and says "I need somebody to run some stuff over to motor pool, but I see you're still working up the stats for our report. I'll get Jameson on it." That's shamming.

Suppose you're sitting at your desk doing nothing, and the first sergeant comes in and says "I need somebody to run over to the motor pool. You wouldn't want to do that, would you?" You say, "Naw." And he says, "OK. I'll get Jameson on it." That's getting over.

Anybody can sham, but getting over is something different. Sometimes it's skill. Sometimes it's luck. Whichever, if you're getting over, everybody envies you.

Getting over is when you get a doctor's slip that says you have foot problems and you can't stand still for long periods of time, so guard duty is out. But moving around is good for you, so you should definitely be assigned to play on the unit basketball team. Practice is during duty hours.

Getting over is when the CO lets you call him Bob.

Getting over is when you leave for a three-day vacation on Thursday afternoon without putting in any papers and on Friday nobody notices you're not at work, or if they do, they don't care.

Getting over is when you only go to the field as part of the IG team.

A lot of people may think you're getting over just because of the job you have. Maybe you are and maybe you aren't. It all depends on your perspective.

Soldiers who work in offices all day think that people who go to the field all the time are getting over, because they don't have to do paperwork.

Soldiers who go to the field all the time think that soldiers who stay in garrison are getting over, because all the fun is back in garrison.

If you're really getting over, you've got a job where you don't have to be in the office very much and you hardly ever go to the field. You've got a job where nobody knows for sure just where you're supposed to be, so you can be wherever you prefer to go. And nobody can say a thing about it.

Getting over is when you can't go to the field because you've got an ironclad appointment with finance on departure day.

Getting over is when you live in an apartment without a telephone, so you can never be notified when there's an alert.

When two units are at the same training site in the field, the soldiers in each unit always figure the soldiers in the other unit are getting over, because they've clearly got less work to do.

You've got to consider who's telling you that somebody's getting over.

If a soldier says an officer is getting over, it may not be true. Most soldiers figure most officers are getting over just by being officers, and they're *really* getting over when they don't come to work because they've gone TDY to some beautiful place.

If a soldier says another soldier is getting over it's probably true. Most soldiers know what getting over is when they see it.

You never hear an officer say that another officer is getting over. They say he's "retired on the job."

Basically, if it's you who's doing it, it isn't getting over. It's only getting over when it's that guy over there.

On Line

Once you take up the military life, whether on active duty, as a civilian employee or dependent, one thing becomes certain. You're going to have to get used to standing in line. Wherever you go, whatever you need to do, at least two hundred people are doing the same thing at the same place and the same time. Most of them are standing in front of you. Single file.

But standing on line isn't all bad. There are lots of things you can do to pass the time, even make it interesting.

Here are just a few:

Figure out your pay per minute. Divide your base pay by 52, then by 40, then by 60. It's OK to use a calculator, but do it in your head if you like a challenge. The figure you get is what your salary is per minute. Did you sneak out of your office to stand in line on work time? Now you know how much per minute Uncle Sam is actually paying you to wait. Feel good? Figure it all out again to make sure, and then feel better.

Sneak a peek at the next guy's checkbook. Can you see the balance? Is it a lot more than yours? Look at him and try to imagine why. Maybe he's a senior officer, or unmarried, or just real smart. Look at him closely and see if you can figure it out. If not, go ahead and ask, politely. "So where d'ja get the dough?"

Practice all the places you can carry your fatigue cap and see which one makes you look the most cool. Put it in your belt. In front. In back. Stick it in your pocket. Shove it down your boot. Put it down the front of your shirt and see if you can make it flat enough so that it's unnoticeable.

Listen to conversations. Stand very still with your ear tilted toward the speaker, but so they can't tell you're eavesdropping. Turn around in a circle until you pick up the best conversation. Listen until you hear them say something really nasty about someone, then say, "Hey! That's my best friend you're talking about!" See if they take the comment back.

Remember everybody you've ever dated. Remember each date, one by one, what your date looked like, what you liked best about that person. Who was the best kisser? Imagine what the perfect date would look like. Imagine the perfect kiss. Does this make you feel sexy? It's fun to feel sexy in the line at the PX because it's so unusual. If you feel too sexy, start thinking about something else.

Look at the junk people are buying in the commissary. Look at the carts of the people standing around you in line, and notice which items are a total waste. Try to total how much money they are spending on plastic food, and imagine what they are going to look like after a few short years of eating that schlock. Feel superior.

Read the ingredients in a can of soup. Count how many there are. How many have you ever heard of before? How many have you ever seen or tasted? What is monosodium glutamate? Is that the same stuff they put in gunpowder? Ask the person in line next to you.

In the dispensary, try to guess the illnesses of the people waiting with you. See who looks feverish. Is anybody moaning in pain? Anybody bleeding? Look carefully at everybody to see if they have any spots. Try to figure out if that man's arm is broken, or does it just naturally bend that funny way?

Plan the entire rest of your life. What grade will you be five years from now? Ten? How much money will you be making? Will you be married to somebody who is rich, tough, and good-looking? Plan your whole future. If that gets too complicated, plan tomorrow afternoon.

Hope that you won't be somewhere standing in line.

The Uniform Code

There are some nasty people who like to go around claiming that Military Intelligence is a contradiction in terms, but they flat don't know what they're talking about. Military people are smarter than ever, and you can see it in a thousand different ways. Take, for example, the fact that everybody knows how to dress themselves correctly.

Oh ho, you're thinking, this is a joke. It's not a joke. If you think it's a joke, then go on over to your local MOS library and have a look at my favorite regulation. This is AR 670-1, "Wear and Appearance of Army Uniform and Insignia." If you can figure this baby out, then you must be some kind of a muscle mind.

And most people do figure it out. Although there are a few good people out there who never have been able to get it quite right.

Once I knew this officer—okay, okay, he was a doctor and we all know we've got to cut doctors some slack—anyway, he had two Class A blouses. When he first came into the service he had somebody put all the insignia on each jacket for him.

He lived on post and walked to work. Every morning he'd walk to the office and hang up the blouse. Every afternoon he'd put it on for the walk home. He lived in deathly fear of spilling something or getting promoted. He knew he could never get the brass back on if he had to take it off for any reason.

I used to chuckle at him, but that was before I'd tried to sew unit patches on fatigue jackets. Anyone who's ever tried to put those thicknesses together one-half of an inch from a shoulder seam knows that AR 670-1 is a force to be respected.

People who haven't thought the thing through probably figure you don't have to be able to read and understand the regulation in order to know how to dress correctly. They think all you have to do is put yourself together like all the people around you and you'll be right. But the fact is, that's a very dangerous way to operate.

Say, for instance, you're strolling around post and you notice a female soldier lined up for inspection with her BDU shirt hanging out. You might think it's okay to give up your belt. But it wouldn't be, because the woman you just saw was wearing the maternity BDU (battle dress uniform). One nice thing about the Army is that they make special uniform exceptions for special situations. Like, pregnant soldiers don't have to wear belts.

I have to admit, I haven't really read 670-1 in detail since the last time the umbrella question came up. It's tough enough to keep up with the changes and amendments.

I hope you know, for instance, that you've been given a reprieve on your olive green undershirts. All you people who look your best in OD have probably been dreading the switch to yuck brown. But now you can wear your beloved greenies for another year, so I hope you haven't let them go to tatters.

And you sunglass-wearers. The new AR says that "individuals who are required by medical authority to wear sunglasses for medical reasons other than refractive error, may wear them except when safety considerations apply." What that means is that you can't wear sunglasses except when the commanding officer says you can. And if you do get permission to wear them, they'd better be the dinky Army kind and not something good-looking.

Actually, quite a few changes to 670-1 have just come out, and you and the first sergeant and the commanding officer are going to have a lot of fun trying to decide what you should put on every day. It will be a real sign of intelligence if you get it right.

You know, it's a funny thing. Some people are so preoccupied with questions like, what went wrong with Sgt. York, and should we restructure the joint chiefs, and how can we cut $2 billion from the defense budget. They don't know that the really burning issues in the military are, what color is your undershirt, and is it okay to wear buckle or zip boots and do your BDUs make you sweat?

Some people think they know a lot, when they really don't know anything.

Milspeak

One of the big challenges of coming over to Germany from CONUS, for both military and civilian personnel, is the language barrier.

I was talking about the problem with a new 71-Q just the other day. "With a journalism MOS," he told me, "I never dreamed I'd have such difficulties with what is basically just a variation of the English language. I mean, I passed my SQT with flying colors. But the minute I hit USAREUR I could see this was another world.

"My wife has had troubles ever since the day we PCSed. She had to take care of the arrangements with our POV, for instance, and she was beginning to feel like my SSAN is her whole identity. Getting the kids set up in DODDS wasn't so simple either.

"But the major problem came when she took her SF-171 in to CPO. She applied for positions in all categories—GS, AS, and UA, but since she's never been SKAPed she had to take a job at a fairly low grade. She wound up in ITO, which is all right, but if she could have gotten something with the local MILCOM I think she would have been happier. PAO is more interesting, and even if she'd gone with MSAD she would have felt more personal involvement.

"Her office has a major shortage of 71-Ls. Half the limas who are assigned there haven't finished BSEP, and the other half are out all day at ESL.

"Still, we got lucky with HRO and were set up in quarters while I was still on TLA. I could have come over earlier on MAC and stayed in the Q, but we were willing to take the risk.

"Lately I've been TDY to V Corps practically all the time, so it's good my wife is working. And the USO has a full program here, so with that entertainment and trips with ITT she stays occupied.

"My job with ACRODOD is working out well. Our biggest activity so far, our ARTEP, was watched pretty closely by the ADC. Unfortunately, right in the middle of it several DRs popped up, including a DWI by the PSG. I'm praying the LT won't come down too hard on my section and try to blame us for the SNAFU, especially since my last EER was only mediocre.

"I work for a terrific SGM, he's really A-OK. When JUMPS screwed up my LES he called HQ on it right away. He'd do the same for any E-deuce. But the 11-bush types are making him a little crazy—he's a 74-F at heart and it's a different world. He says we'll have to look for him in CDAAC if DA doesn't put the right position on his TDA.

"The previous NCOIC, now DFR, ETSed out of sheer frustration. He even sent the IG and DF asking for an ROI on the communication problem. But in the last few weeks before he DEROSed his attitude was strictly FIGMO, so nothing happened.

"I tried to follow up, but my POC got transferred over to RMO to work out the AF budget CAD. I even asked the JAG if there was any sort of AR on clarity, but he was temporarily out of the AO.

"Right now I'm just trying to get a DA-31 approved so I can get down to AFRC for some R&R.

"Eventually, I hope to get an ITT to EUCOM, maybe even work

for the CINC somehow. I'd like to be able to make some input to the SGS there about a possible SOP on clear communication. Everybody here is so used to milspeak they've forgotten how to talk right.

"It was never like this in FORSCOM."

Mind over Matter

The main thing to remember about taking the PT test is that it's all in your head. Think positive—that's the key. Too many people let themselves get psyched out by the idea of the test, and once that happens, they're doomed.

Sure it's true you're not quite as young as you used to be. That doesn't matter. Take a look at the young troops around. See how frivolous, how superficial they are. Never a thought for tomorrow. Never a thought for what happens outside their own little worlds. You are not like that. You are experienced, mature. You bring a wealth of wisdom to all your undertakings—wisdom you have gained by living through situations and knowing what really counts. So why are you so worried about the PT test?

Your approach, of course, must be somewhat different from that of more junior people. They keep fit by chasing after members of the opposite sex, by carousing until dawn, by engaging in the repetitive lifting of mailbags or ammo boxes or tool kits or whatever.

You have long since grown beyond such simple activities. So while others may bring a certain youthful vigor to the tests, you are well aware that this vigor is theirs only through an idiosyncrasy of nature, and not through any personal merit. You, on the other hand, approach the PT test equipped with the same superior qualities that you bring to all your professional activities. A broad vision, maturity, experience, and a self-confidence that is well deserved.

Thus, your preparation for this semiannual event must take an appropriately dignified form.

First, consider the requirements. They are almost laughable: a short run, big deal. Recall the many times in your distinguished career when you have run longer distances under far more stressful conditions in half the time. Think back to when you coached the boys' soccer team. Good grief, you did some running then! All afternoon, up and down the field, never a moment for a break.

Take a look at the course over which the run will take place. Walk around it if you like, perhaps take an easy jog. Study the ground. Imagine yourself running two or three quick laps; think about how easy and even invigorating such a run can be. Let the certainty pervade your mind. The run will be no problem.

Think about the sit-ups. What could be easier than sit-ups? Glance through a few fitness books next time you're in the PX. Notice that every book includes sit-ups, even for those who are just embarking on a fitness program for the first time in their lives. Sit-ups are a beginner's exercise. Anyone can do them.

If you find yourself building up a moderate interest in exercise, take some time to watch one of the new videotapes or exercise programs on TV. Watch the cute young instructors in their leotards doing sit-ups with virtually no effort at all. Picture yourself doing the sit-ups. Think about how you would maintain a quick, steady rhythm. Picture yourself and the trim exercise instructor doing sit-ups together.

But what about push-ups? Push-ups may seem harder, but it's all in your attitude. Think positive. Look at your arms. Notice the muscle on the top and the other one on the bottom. Flex the muscles and ask your spouse or another loved one to feel them. Bask in the appreciation.

If you have some spare time, drop by the gym and watch the people working out with weights. Observe one of the companies in your battalion doing PT. Note their technique on the push-ups and sit-ups. Imagine yourself right in there with them, doing all those exercises, keeping up with the best of them, barely breathing hard, not sweating at all.

It's all mental. Think positive and you've got it made. It's easy.

Comes the day of the PT test. You're set. Remember all the positive images of yourself you've been visualizing? Now all you've got to do is get out there and make it happen.

Specializing

Pretty soon now, there will be no more specialists. Next month about 46,000, give or take a few, will more or less vanish into the ether.

I feel kind of sorry about this. For one thing, I've had quite a few friends who were specialists. And each of them really was special, in his or her own way. It's a charming system, but one that's hard to appreciate if you've never known anything else.

Just to give you some perspective, I have a friend who works in an interservice situation. Some new Navy staff people showed up one day, and he naturally asked them what their specialties were. "Specialties?" they said, looking confused. Turned out they didn't have any specialties. They were able-bodied and that was about it.

I don't mean to sound negative about being able-bodied. I think it's a great thing. But it's not like being a specialist. Being able-bodied is better than the alternative, but it can't compare with being special.

I bet a lot of the 46,000 specialists don't realize what they're losing. They probably think it will be neat to become sergeants and such. That's because sergeants get all the glamour. When you say someone's a sergeant, the whole world knows what you're talking about. A sergeant is tough. A sergeant is experienced. A sergeant doesn't have to play up to anybody. He isn't handicapped by wimpish personal ambition. He isn't wet behind the ears and naive.

Sergeants are okay, but it's the movies that have mostly fostered this mucho macho image. What was Rambo? I haven't seen the movie, but I bet he was a sergeant. I just have this funny feeling he wasn't a Spec 5. That's because people don't think of a specialist as being particularly good at holding up under torture or ruthlessly annihilating the enemy and crusading for pure justice. The fact is, most people don't think about specialists at all.

The Army isn't getting rid of all its specialists. It's keeping Spec 4s. But what kind of system is that? Some Spec 4s will still be made into corporals. And the others will know that no matter what, no matter how hard they devote themselves to their specialties, they can never become Spec 5s, much less Spec 6s. They can only move on to become tough, hard-bitten sergeants.

Personally, I always had confidence when dealing with a specialist. I've had the feeling that most of these people actually knew what they were doing. That they could be trusted to accomplish the job.

I'll agree that when it comes to taking Hill 247 a sergeant is probably the person for the job. But when I go to seek legal advice or eat at the dining facility or get my teeth cleaned I'd rather deal with a specialist.

I have always felt rather proud of knowing a little something about specialists. Most civilians have never even heard of the grade, and on those occasions when it comes up in casual conversation, I've always been quick to explain that a specialist is not a sergeant, is not like a sergeant, is really something else altogether. Something—dare I say it—something rather better than a sergeant.

More interesting and precious.

That, at least, is the way I see it.

I find a disturbing aspect to the Armywide elimination of the key specialist grades. Without specialists, who will take care of all the various specialties? Who will do the jobs that require someone special? Every specialist knows—and I've heard many of them say it many times—that there's no sergeant around who can handle a specialist's responsibilities.

I have a strong feeling that the 46,000 new sergeants are going to be about as popular as the new Coke. That there will be a hue and cry to bring back the days of old when specialties were handled by specialists. But the Army isn't like a big corporation. It's not likely to switch back to the old way. And sooner or later people will get used to the fact that everybody's a sergeant. Which is about like being able-bodied.

I think that's too bad. I like the way things are now.

I think they're kind of special.

Paying Up

This is the time of year when I really start feeling my oats. It always happens when I fill out those tax forms and ship them off. Many people live lives replete with deductions, but not me. I pay up every year, and I pay big bucks. We're talking stratospheric here. Like, there have been years when I held a regular job that we had to give my whole salary back. All of it.

Some people find this depressing. That's because they don't understand the system. They think their money goes into a Black Hole in Washington, D.C., and vanishes into the ether. That's not the way I look at it.

I feel really good when I think about just what it is my money buys. In fact, I feel powerful. For instance, part of my money goes to pay a general's salary for one week. I've asked the U.S. Government to see to it that our local general is the recipient of my personal largess. I like to call him up at work and remind him of this fact.

"So, hi, General," I say, after I've gotten him on the line by telling his secretary that "The Boss" is calling. "What are you up to today?"

"Who is this?" he demands, not yet comprehending the situation.

"This is the person who's paying your salary this week," I say sternly. "And I want to know what you're doing on my time."

"Ah, certainly," he says with the nervous edge military people get when they're talking to someone who's more in charge than they are. "Well, actually I'm working on the agenda for a weapons conference in Paris."

"Cancel it," I snap. "Last year the Paris conference used up all the tax dollars I wanted to spend on the women's locker room at our gym. Do Paris on somebody else's week."

"All right," the General agrees with some reluctance. "I do need to update the post beautification program and get rolling on the Holiday Ball."

"Sounds good," I tell him. "But don't take the next 51 weeks too easy. Remember: I'll be calling again next year."

Once I get the General squared away I try to take care of the other areas where my money goes. For instance, I've specifically asked my congressman to arrange for my monies to be spent in the post library. So along about now I usually deliver my list of recommended new acquisitions.

"I don't know about this," said the librarian when she saw this year's request. "We already have over 20 dog-training books on the shelves."

"None of them works," I tell her briskly. "I've read them all and my dog still . . . you know. In the house."

"I see," she says uncertainly. "Maybe we can get these."

"Maybe isn't good enough," I snarl. "Keep in mind that next year I'm switching my money from the NASA program to your salary. For one week, you'll be working directly for me."

"I won't forget," she answers meekly.

Some of my money goes to benefit soldiers and their families in very direct ways. For instance, I earmarked a goodly sum for improvement of quarters in Germany. You can imagine how horrified I was on a recent visit when I noticed workmen painting a series of stairwells an unpleasant shade of river-bottom green. "Stop that right now," I exhorted them.

"*Was ist los?*" asked the foreman.

"That's an awful color," I told him. "My specific tax dollars are paying for that, and I don't like it. I don't want my name associated with it. Take it back and use something else. Paint these apartments a nice blue."

"Okay," said the workman, once a translator had made my position clear. "I will do as you say because you are in charge."

I've been very particular about how I want my money spent. I've asked that it be used only to support field kitchens, for example, and not to buy any MREs.

I've requested that it be spent only on new uniform items being made of Goretex, and not a penny for BDUs.

And I've indicated that my dollars must be used to purchase only quartermaster items that are attractive and tasteful. Let somebody else pay for the tacky stuff.

The problem is that I contribute so much money every year that it has to be spread around to a lot of different places, and there's no way I can keep on top of them all. It's frankly impossible for me to carry out the kind of quality control I'd like to do.

But just about this time every year I have a real good time trying.

3

Colonels' Wives and Other Dubious Phenomena

The Colonel's Wife

Somewhere, somehow, some colonel's wife is doing a number on us all. I've been hearing about her for years, but I've never thought of actually doing anything. Well, it's all finally gotten to be too much. It's time to find this woman and shake some sense into her.

Surely you've heard about her.

She's the one who's directly responsible for two barracks buildings of soldiers spending an entire weekend doing cleanup duty. Apparently, she was walking past the area on her way to some luncheon when she noticed a couple of beer cans lying on the ground. A couple of beer cans! Well, wouldn't you know she got the wind up and mentioned it to her husband who mentioned it to the CG and the next thing you know it was scrub-down time.

Everybody knows that the colonel himself couldn't have cared less. He understands how these things happen, and he knows how to take care of a little trash in a quiet way. So when two beer cans add up to weekend duty for everybody, you know exactly who's really behind it.

Then there was the business of the party at the rec center. It was just a matter of borrowing a few tables and chairs from the chapel on a Saturday night so a few troops would have a little celebration. Nothing wild, just a little song, a little dance, a little drink and eat. And a few extra tables and chairs so a person could sit down.

Well, of course, the official word was that the chaplain didn't want to lend things out, but the real story is that some colonel's wife was having a coffee the next morning and she was afraid the stuff wouldn't get returned in time.

The wives can sit and talk about this woman all day long. She's had them quaking in their boots ever since she got the major transferred. You've heard that stuff like that doesn't happen anymore, but in this case it sure did. The major was really an OK guy, but his wife and some colonel's wife didn't get along at all. There are a lot of different versions about exactly what went down, but the bottom line is that one day the major was there, like always, and the next day he was gone. Reassigned in a flash to Fort Polk or some place like that. And some colonel's wife was behind the whole thing.

This woman spends about 90 percent of her time out shopping. She singlehandedly keeps the PX and the commissary depleted of practically anything you might want to buy. It seems like anytime you ask for something that isn't on the shelf it turns out some colonel's wife just bought up a shipment's worth. That's not what the manager says, of course. He tells you it's on order, just like he always says. But if you look around, maybe chat with the clerks now and then, you'll find out the truth.

If something's all out, it's pretty certain that some colonel's wife has been loading up.

She's even made a mess out of the parking situation here. It's always crowded, but there used to be a couple of places where you could squeeze a car in right up front. Just give it a try now though, and see where it gets you. "You can't park here," is all the MPs will tell you, but it doesn't take many brains to see the real reason why.

Some colonel's wife complained.

The fact is, the more you look around, the more you notice how things get really messed up because some colonel's wife had to put in her two cents' worth. And the thing that's so amazing is that the colonel himself is a terrific person. It's only his wife who's running amok.

You don't actually see her around much, but you sure do hear the stories.

After everything she's done for us, I'd like to repay the favor by giving her a good-sized piece of my mind.

Article 15

It may sound cruel, but the office took up a pool on what the kid's punishment might be. Twenty minutes before he went down for his Article 15 hearing, everybody put in a dollar and made a guess. The idea was that if anybody hit it, they would get the money.

In a way it kind of eased the tension for him. The laughing and the black humor helped put it in perspective, helped him realize that it was actually happening. Because in spite of himself he couldn't quite believe his number was really up.

Not that an Article 15 is that big a deal. People get them all the time. Sometimes they don't even stay permanently on your record. Sometimes you just get a letter of reprimand. Some people look at them as something akin to a badge of honor. You're not a real man unless you've had at least one. That sort of thinking is common.

But the kid is used to having a clean record. He's used to smiling his way out of trouble. The forlorn look, the sincere apology, the 'gee whiz, I didn't know it was wrong'—these are the techniques that had saved him before.

Still, after a while, smile and guile don't do it anymore. And the day that happens is the day a guy finds out what facing the music is really all about.

In this case, it's got to be said, the kid simply didn't play it right.

The cause of the hullabaloo was a little matter of eight days AWOL. It was leave time that had gotten a little out of hand. Circumstances contributed to the difficulties of the kid's return, and the way things worked out he got his ride home from the airport from a couple of MPs in uniform.

He'd gone to visit his wife, who is stationed in a distant place. He calls her "wife." "Bride" would be a better word. He only knew her a few weeks before they were married; only spent two days with her after the ceremony. Then he came here and she went there and this leave was their first reunion since.

Plans went awry when his originally scheduled flight back was canceled. Over the busy holiday season no other seat could be confirmed for days. He called home base and asked for an extension of his leave. It was denied.

So rather than spend some miserable days waiting standby at a crowded airport, he sank into a long week of noncommunicative connubial bliss.

His unit gave him 48 hours of leave and then dropped him AWOL.

If he had come back with a story of passion — "Sarge, I had to be with her just a few more days!" — it's tough to imagine that even a hardened NCO wouldn't have sympathized.

"I couldn't leave her just yet," is what he should have said. "I know it was wrong, and I'm ready to take my punishment. It was worth it."

That's not the tack he took. Instead he told a tale of bungled messages, of signing in with an individual whose identity remained vague, of proof positive that would be coming via military channels.

Twelve days later nothing had turned up. Twelve days of apprehension, suspense, gossip, and ever-growing needling from his coworkers.

"Have you told the CO your story?" someone asked him shortly before the official inquisition.

"Yes," he nodded briskly.

His questioner shook her head. "Then you're sunk for sure."

His immediate supervisor cross-examined him relentlessly, to help prepare him for the ordeal, but in the end announced that the story was not improving with age.

At the hearing, which was open in order to allow for the admission of evidence (of which there was none), the officers saw it the same way. No matter how you looked at it, the kid had not been where he was supposed to be. He had not called to say why. He was AWOL without a doubt.

They gave him a bust, small fine, two weeks of extra duty. And a fifteen-day appeal period in case some evidence to support his story should appear.

Back at the office it turned out that nobody's guess on the punishment had hit the mark, so the kid was awarded the money.

Six bucks and a dose of reality, just at a time when both were badly needed.

A Fan

Just when those of us who live in Germany were beginning to wonder how welcome we really are here, along came Michael Dombert and made us feel as if maybe we were getting the wrong idea.

Michael is a 17-year-old German. He works as a baker's apprentice. He likes Americans a lot. And he likes American soldiers even more. He likes them so much that, more than anything in the whole wide world, he wishes he were a soldier in the U.S. Army.

The U.S. military sponsors a system of clubs for young Americans and Germans who want to get to know each other. They're called *Kontakt* clubs, and they are popular—run by young people for young people. They offer a variety of activities both on and off post, where people like Dombert can get to know soldiers. Germans who join *Kontakt* clubs often are given special, limited passes to Army posts, so that they can participate fully.

But that wasn't really what Michael Dombert had in mind. He didn't want to just get to know American soldiers. He wanted to really be one—in his fantasies, at least. And after a while, those fantasies became too hard to resist.

So Dombert went to a flea market and bought an old pair of fatigues. He got some American friends to buy him boots and insignia. He made himself an E-5.

And then he began to make regular visits to Cambrai-Fritsch Kaserne, a U.S. Army post in Darmstadt. At a time when strict antiterrorist measures limit post access and call for 100 percent ID checks, Dombert wandered on and off post almost at will.

"I never kept count of how many times I was on the *kaserne*," he told reporters later, "but one hundred times is definitely a low estimate."

He didn't do much while he was wandering around the small post. He didn't go in any buildings. He didn't take anything or do any damage. "It was just good to be there," he said. "I was afraid to talk to anybody because my English isn't very good. Some of the younger soldiers would say, 'Sir' to me when I passed by and that made me feel good."

Michael's fantasy unraveled late one Friday afternoon. He was walking about the post as usual. He had been especially adventurous that week, visiting the post three days in a row. He was walking just ahead of a small group of soldiers when he suddenly realized they had all just saluted smartly. A major had walked by, and, despite the sometimes casual air in today's Army, Dombert's omission was painfully apparent. The major asked Dombert why he had not saluted, and Michael found, to his horror, that he could not get a word out. The major asked for his ID card. But Dombert did not have an ID card. He was escorted to the MP station.

The community went on high security alert. Notifications were made. Guards around the general's house were increased. And people hearing about the incident secondhand began wondering. Was this a terrorist penetration? Was the bogus soldier a scout for some group with evil deeds in mind? Had the key to a spy ring been uncovered?

It wasn't any of those things, of course. It was just Michael Dombert, baker's apprentice, making his usual rounds on the American post. The MPs turned him over to the German police, who sent him home.

"Thank God the Americans can take a joke," said Dombert's father.

Meanwhile, the Americans were still wondering, how did Dombert get on post all those times without an ID card? Dombert said it was simple. The gate guards at Cambrai-Fritsch Kaserne are primarily civilians. Said Dombert, "It was only a problem when the older guards were on duty. They even checked the ID cards of the uniformed soldiers. But I was never asked because I avoided them."

Dombert's story left Americans with divided opinions. What do you do about such a young man? Do you punish him for pretending to be what he isn't? Or do you give him a reward, send him to visit a unit for a day, try to encourage his positive views of the U.S. Army?

So far, nobody has done much of anything. But there may still be a chance. Michael Dombert promises he'll be back.

Command Desire

People who've been around the military any time at all know that, for officers, command isn't everything. It's the only thing. Sure, you've got your glamour commands, the big brigades, and the hot action units. But even if training commands or community commands draw snickers from the sidelines, they're still command opportunities. They give an officer a chance to actually accomplish something, like change the rec center hours, by merely dropping a word.

An officer who's not in command is a man (or woman) who's a menace. Because if there's one thing in this world that's sad to see, it's an office full of colonels sitting around pretending to be in charge of something. After all those years of leadership training, they can't help but constantly be on the lookout for followers.

If you have to live with somebody like this you know what I'm talking about. It's Command Desire Syndrome — CDS — and you can recognize it easily. Just ask yourself a few simple questions.

Does your spouse encourage the family to engage in sports together? Does he make everybody weigh in? Does he insist that you jog together in formation? These typical CDS symptoms are bearable, but watch out. Does he test you with skin calipers "just for fun?" Is he designing a family guidon? The syndrome could be getting out of hand.

What about his behavior around the house? Does he demand that all books and records be organized alphabetically and an author/artist index cross reference be kept handy? Does he inspect your quarters at unannounced times? If you fail inspection, does he make you run around the block with the baby in a knapsack?

Some of the syndrome indicators may be more subtle. How, for instance, does he want you to answer the telephone? Is it okay to say "Hello?" Certainly, there's nothing unnatural if he suggests you answer the phone by giving the family name. But does he also ask you to list your status in life, your address, and other vital statistics? If he wants you to say, "Fenwick quarters, Mary Fenwick, current wife, speaking; 'Fenwicks Fit, Fast, and First' is our motto, may I help you SIR!'" don't do it. It's liable to make people think you're the one who's nuts.

For some who've got CDS really bad, the symptoms can expand and worsen. Does he make you route the grocery list to him in advance for his approval? Does he insist that it be submitted in triplicate? Does he refuse to okay it unless it's been initialed by each of the kids?

When you go out, does he sit in the back seat while you drive? Does he wait for you to open the car door? Does he have safety and maintenance rules posted all over the dashboard? Is he making a little sign with the family crest on it to put in the windshield?

Is he constantly asking you to brief him on the status of the situation at the children's school? In the laundry room? With the milkman? Does he complain if your presentation is not accompanied by an audiovisual display?

Does he refuse to fool around unless you have a security clearance? Does he like it best when you war-game new maneuvers? Are his jammies olive drab?

Does he insist that the children all dress identically, even though the youngest is in kindergarten and the oldest is a senior? Does he expect everyone to stand up when he comes to the dinner table? When he enters any room? When he's somewhere in the house?

Does he encourage the children to get together with their neighborhood friends and play "Parade"? Does he stand outside at attention when they do?

If you're living with an officer who is exhibiting these symptoms, you must be warned: There is no cure. The only hope for you is if he's given a chance to transfer his attentions to the troops.

So, in case you're one of those who doesn't much care whether your spouse goes into a command slot, perhaps you'd better change your attitude.

A new view could save your sanity.

Oh, Poop

I am tired of getting blamed for all the dog poops in my neighborhood. Many of these poops have nothing to do with me or with my dog. The first time I have seen most of them is that ugly moment when the portiere, our compound groundskeeper, accosts me on my usual walk and leads me to the latest evidence. "Signora," is all he says. His raised eyebrow speaks the rest of the message.

So how am I to respond? "I have never seen that before," has been my usual answer. But I can plainly see the portiere is unconvinced.

This issue took on an especially cruel aspect last summer when anonymous charges were brought against me. One day the portiere appeared at my door to inform me that I would no longer be allowed to walk my dog within the confines of our *parco*. "It is the decision of the administration," he intoned solemnly. "It is for cleanliness' sake."

Well, okay. When I first moved in I used to clean up my dog's poop assiduously. I admit I grew lax, but I had my reasons.

Reason #1. My neighborhood is inhabited by at least 50 unowned cats that roam, mess, get into garbage, and do as they please when they please. No one complains, because they keep the rats down.

Reason #2. My neighborhood is surrounded by packs of stray dogs that invade our *parco* whenever an owned dog goes into heat.

Reason #3. It is the portiere's job to sweep the road daily. He does this willingly, cleaning up all kinds of odious refuse, but there is nothing that he finds so offensive as a poop purportedly left by a small domesticated dog.

So, I made a deal. I agreed to clean up after my dog without fail, in return for the privilege of being allowed to take him out. This cleanup is accomplished by means of a small cat litter scoop that I use to launch the excretia over our fence into a garbage dump on one side, or a large orchard on the other.

Still there were complaints. "You shouldn't throw that stuff into the farmer's field," sniffed one neighbor, despite the fact that said farmer twice yearly hauls in two tons of water buffalo leavings, which in turn attract enough flies to block out the noonday sun.

"If the orchard's out," I told my neighbor, "then how about I dump it in your yard? So far as I can tell you haven't mowed since the Allies invaded Italy, so I'm sure you'd never notice."

But such smart remarks are not the answer, and this place is not the only one where the problem exists. In Germany I lived in government quarters and everyone agreed that a certain section of grass would be designated "Poop Platz." Nothing was barred there, but a small field where the children played was a definite no go.

The only problem was that it's hard to teach a dog such fine points of behavior, and the Germans, who love dogs more than children, totally refused to cooperate.

Personally, I don't mind cleaning up after my own dog at all. I do a regular poop patrol in my small, fenced yard. And I have my trusty scoop ready whenever we are about in the neighborhood.

Educating others is the real problem. I am highly visible, because I am the only resident to take a dog on regular, supervised walks. It doesn't seem to occur to people that a lot of poops are left by dogs that were out running around loose. When people in my neighborhood see a poop on the street, they think of me, which isn't fair at all.

In fact the whole situation has turned me into a very sensitive person. I dread coming across stray poops, but I can spot them at fifty paces. And since every poop I see represents a nasty thought that someone has had about me, they make me feel most melancholy. Why, even my dreams are invaded by

Ghoulies and ghosties
and long-leggety beasties
and things that go 'poop' in the night.

The Meetin' and Greetin' Colonel

You could call him the meetin' and greetin' colonel. That's what he likes to do. He likes to meet the new folks in his community, and he likes to greet them when he sees them on the street.

"People see me in civilian clothes and they know who I am," he says with pride. "Soldiers see me on the street and they say 'Hi.'"

They know him from the orientation briefing he gives the new arrivals every week or so. It's a heaven or hellfire all-American booster talk that would do Billy Graham proud.

The colonel can make you a believer.

On the way to the briefing, he speaks enthusiastically about the orientation program. "I want to tell the soldiers that I'm glad they're here. I want 'em to know they're welcome.

"Every week I get three or four written comments from soldiers in this community. I see that those questions are answered and a letter is sent to that soldier, signed by me. Personally."

The colonel bursts into the room where forty soldiers sit waiting. "Hey! Isn't it great to be alive!" he shouts. "Let me hear it!"

"It's great to be alive!" the forty soldiers shout back.

"Let me tell you why I'm here. I'm here because when I first got to this community, you know what I saw? I saw soldiers gettin' drunk, goofin' off, who didn't give a damn to be a soldier in the U.S. Army. And I decided, I'm gonna talk to those soldiers, and I'm gonna see if it can help. And it's helped.

"You're here and you feel down," cried the colonel. "You got no pay, no transport, and you haven't had a joint in six days and you think you've got problems. Well, let me tell you something. Those are little tiny problems. You know why? I'll tell you why. It's because we're glad you're here. And you've got three beautiful things going for you.

"One, you're an American. You've got so much. Think about the guy that can't get a hot shower or never hears a toilet flush. Think about your freedoms. Your problems are so small.

"Two, you're a soldier in the U.S. Army. Anybody ever tell you that's a beautiful thing? Well it is, because it's a world championship team and you're a member. If our president wants us to, we can do anything. We can send anybody anywhere anytime if we have to. If the president wanted us to send in a team and take over the Kremlin for twenty-four hours we could do that.

"No other country can do that. Not even Israel.

"I'm a winner. I don't like to lose. I never trained a day in my life to take second place. I don't want to go to war and take second place.

"The third beautiful thing is that you've been assigned to this community. There are thirty-nine military communities in Germany. This one's the best. It's the best 'cause I say it's best. I wouldn't have it any other way. I'm a winner.

"You've got these three beautiful things going for you. So what are a few little problems? When you're that good, there's no little problem you can't lick. And we're here to help you do it.

"I'm in charge around here. See all those vehicles painted with camouflage colors? I'm not in charge of those. See everything else? I'm in charge.

"We're doing things in this community. I'm the guy that's doing them. My job is to make you happy. I want you to be a winner.

"Whatever it takes for you to come to work with a smile on your face and a spring in your step, that's what I'm going to do.

"I've asked for a swimming pool. With Congress' approval it's gonna be built in five years. Don't laugh. If some guy had done that twenty years ago, we'd have that pool today. I'm gonna come back in five years and take a damn swim.

"So when you get lonely and you start thinking that nobody loves you no more, I want you to remember me. And know that somebody does.

"Think of a soldier you know. A soldier that's been in the Army as long as you have, that's in your grade, that's in your MOS. Know anybody like that that can do your job better than you can? Of course not. You know some that are good, but not that good.

"The unit you're assigned to is a better unit because it's got you. You're here because you're winners.

"Units without military discipline and training are losers.

"I want to do everything I can for you. I want you to enjoy it here. You can come to me with suggestions or problems. I want to hear them. I just want to ask two things of you in return.

"I ask you to represent our country well. And be proud you're a soldier.

"I'm a winner, and I think the Army's great."

We Wives Are People, Too

A couple of disturbing things have happened in recent weeks.

First, I reported on a large-scale volunteer project. I spoke at length with an enlisted wife who gave me some fine insight into the work that had been done. One of the project coordinators confirmed my feeling that this particular woman had made a tremendous contribution.

But when I called her back to double-check some details, her frank attitude had changed to one of concerned hesitation. Word of the interview had gotten out, and the result had been a call from the CO's wife. "She wants me to be sure and say you should emphasize the many people who worked on this," said the newly nervous volunteer. "I can give you her number if you'd like to talk to her."

I declined, but when I talked to the volunteer a third time I learned she had received yet another call from yet another helpful officer's wife, trying to make sure that a woman who put in a lot of time on an important project would tell the story in the "right" way.

I was still musing over that one when I got a call from a reporter in Alabama. She's working on a story about military wives and the problems they face when seeking employment. The topic is eternally timely, and I was glad to see a civilian newspaper addressing it.

But the reporter was having trouble finding women willing to discuss their experiences. "I know a lot of military wives," she told me, "but they're afraid to talk. They're afraid of hurting their husbands' careers."

This takes me back to a day I'd thought was happily over, and it also puts a rather mean-spirited slant on a traditional problem. The question is, who are we really afraid of? What a disappointing thing when the answer turns out to be "each other."

The role a military wife plays in her husband's career was hotly debated for years. Some said wifey must work at the Thrift Shop, must host the appropriate social events, must cater to the more senior wives and never forget her place. There are still pockets of resistance where these archaic views hold sway and where a tough hardliner can make life miserable for young soldiers and their wives.

But I think, more often, we do it to ourselves. And sometimes, we do it to each other.

Most colonels' wives I know would be horrified at the thought of younger women jumping to their every suggestion. And yet, so often, that is precisely what happens. We impose on ourselves a fear of what might happen if the CO's wife becomes displeased, if we draw attention to ourselves, if we propose a view, however gently, that might not precisely follow the senior perspective.

We are afraid of . . . what? That our husband won't be promoted. That he will fall out of favor with the hierarchy. That he will always get the weekend duty and that the next assignment will be to the most distant and desolate place imaginable.

I'm not suggesting provoking confrontations. I do know there are a few old birds, nurtured in a different age, who feel a military rank means always being right. I also know there are pressures applied by some husbands who honestly believe the displeasure of a superior's wife can doom the most promising career.

But that's all hogwash. Military people are judged by their performance on the job and, yes, by maintaining appropriate personal standards. I'll never believe my husband's future hinges on my volunteer hours or my slavish attention to the boss's wife or my willingness to give up my freedom of expression. If it does, then I'm afraid his career is doomed.

We wives are people, too. I can think of no reason we should deny ourselves, or deny each other, the simple right to a personal identity.

Can you?

4

The Bare Facts of
Life Overseas

The Bare Facts

I can't understand it. My husband is severely annoyed with me just because I took off all my clothes in front of a bunch of strange German men. And the really galling thing is, none of *them* even gave a hoot.

Blame it all on my friend the Finn. He's a health addict who frequents all the spas. When he told me that many are mixed sex and nude—my curiosity was aroused. Give it a try, Finn recommended. The Germans think nothing of it.

When I told my husband I was thinking of baring all, he had just one question. "Why?"

I explained that it was part of learning about Germany. Part of coming to understand another culture.

"If you want culture, go to a museum," he said. "If you want culture, go to a play or a symphony, or learn flower arranging. Don't go to a nude spa and tell me you're searching for culture. I'm smarter than I look."

But I had made up my mind. I called my friend Prissy to see if she would go with me. Prissy is very attractive, which is to say her shape is exactly the reverse of my own classic pear. I figured if I were standing next to Prissy, nobody would look at me no matter what I had on. Even if it was nothing.

Prissy was lukewarm about the idea at first. "I'll think it over and call you back," she told me. Ten minutes later the phone rang. "When are we going to this nasty place?" Prissy bubbled. "My husband wants to come too!"

I balked. "No way. It's just you and me or not at all." My whole upbringing has centered on the fact that you just don't take your clothes off in front of men you know.

I tried to persuade a few other women on my block to join in the adventure, but came up with no takers. The main reason seemed to be vanity. "Call me back 10 pounds from now," was the common response.

So, on a rainy weekday Prissy and I packed up our towels and bathing suits and headed for a spa suitably far out of our town. We supposed it would be a kind of small, neighborhood place. We supposed on a weekday there wouldn't be many people there. We supposed wrong.

The spa was the size of Shea Stadium, and the parking lot was jammed with thousands of cars. There was a long line of people waiting to get in.

Obviously, word had gotten around that we were going to be there.

As we approached the ticket counter we realized we could have a problem. A variety of entry fees were explained in German. Our limited knowledge of the language did not cover this situation. What ticket to buy?

"We want to be naked," Prissy said loudly to the uninterested clerk. "Three marks extra," came the amazing answer. We had expected a discount.

We changed into swimsuits in a dressing area and entered the main spa. There were whirlpools, massage pools, sunlamps, and a fake beach. Off in a corner was a sign pointing to the nude area.

We strode in casually, handing our tickets over to a young man whose expression was a permanent leer.

People were walking around a garden taking deep breaths. People were lying under sunlamps. A large group was sitting on little stools, soaking their feet in small tubs. They were old and young, in every size and condition. Nobody had any clothes on.

Prissy peeled off her bikini. I followed suit, hesitantly, waiting nervously for a clap of thunder, a shriek from the men in the room, or a sudden appearance by my mother. Nothing happened.

"Sauna's this way," Prissy said, and nonchalantly walked toward the door. I strode directly behind her, walking in perfect step like the good little soldier I am. I was still anticipating some manifestations of divine wrath. In the sauna, about two hundred people sat crowded together on three levels of wooden benches. It was very hot and everyone was sweating. A lot.

"Gee, this is swell," I lied to Prissy. A furtive glance around the small room assured me the men were all as thoroughly relaxed as I was uneasy. Every now and then someone new would come in and people would scooch over to make room. Everybody was very polite.

Unbelievably, nobody gave Prissy a second glance.

Just as I began to fear we might melt away completely, we exited the sauna and joined the hordes taking cold showers in a large, open room. We debated strolling in the garden, but it was rather chilly out for naked people. Enough of a good thing, we decided, and I immediately faced a new problem.

How do you wriggle into a wet one-piece bathing suit in front of several dozen people and still retain a measure of dignity?

The answer is, you don't. You just squeeze yourself in as fast as you can, and then make a quick exit.

Outside, I had to compliment Prissy on her attitude. "You're so calm, so cool," I told her enviously. "I wish I could carry it off like that."

"Why not?" she answered primly. "Without my glasses I'm blind as a bat. Were there any men in there?"

Rendezvous in Russia

His name, he told me, is Alex, but that may not be his real name. I know for certain that he is a lieutenant because he showed me his identity booklet. Proud to make it clear he is an officer, he held it open so I could see his picture. He showed me the word "lieutenant" on the opposite page, but I still could not make out his full name.

I am not familiar with the Russian alphabet.

I met him in a store on Kalininsky Prospekt in Moscow. "I couldn't help but overhear you speaking English," he told me. "I'm wondering—I mean I don't wish to be forward—but it would be good to practice my English. I haven't spoken it in so long. Perhaps we could talk for a while? Perhaps I could be of some assistance to you?"

I hesitated.

"Perhaps you have done some reading in preparation for your trip to Russia?" he asked me.

Yes, I admitted. *The Russians* by Hedrick Smith.

Alex smiled. "I know it well. Smith talks about a store where the elite of Moscow buy. What appears to be just another office but is really a well-stocked shop. That place is just a few steps from here. May I take you there?"

My traveling companion and I debated briefly, but the lure was too great. Yes, we told him. Let's go.

On the way we asked Alex if he felt free to associate openly with foreigners, especially Americans.

He smiled. "It is prohibited because of my work. I am in the Soviet army. But just now I am on leave, and my station is far from here. No one I know will see me.

"You know there is an image, a myth about the KGB. That they are everywhere. That they know everything. But this cannot be true. Anyway, who can stop me from talking with you here on the street?"

And *The Russians?* Is that book available in the Soviet Union?

"It is forbidden," Alex admitted. "But I know several people—perhaps a dozen—who have it. I know the book very well."

We rounded a corner and turned up a narrow side street of tall buildings, much like other side streets of Moscow. Except this street was lined with stretch limousines and black Volgas. "Here is the place," whispered Alex. "Here on our right."

It was a small entrance way, with a plaque giving the name. "Bureau of Passes," Alex translated. A well-dressed man carrying a large bag stepped out, and his chauffeur started the engine.

We hurried past.

"Look," said Alex. "I'd like to ask a favor. Let me read you something from our newspaper. To practice my translation."

He began to read a Soviet review of an American spy film. The Americans were the good guys. The Russians were the bad guys. Alex translated the title of the film as "Meanness and Stupidity."

"The reviewer calls this film a typical example of the hate-mongering campaign against the Soviet Union that is constantly waged by Hollywood," said Alex. "Have you seen this film?"

No, we told him.

"Could such a film truly exist?" he demanded.

Sure, we said. It could be one of many. But it's just an adventure story. There is no hate-mongering campaign in the United States. There are other films with other points of view.

"Ah," said Alex. Then he abruptly changed the subject. "What are you told about Poland?"

Very simply, that Solidarity was becoming a little too capitalistic for the government there.

"Yes! And it is the responsibility of the state to put down anti-Socialist activities."

But we are told that the danger lies in the possibility of Soviet interference.

Alex laughed. "We're told the danger is that the Americans may interfere. I suspect the truth lies somewhere in between."

We had stopped on a street corner to debate a point when Alex noticed a policeman looking our way. "Let's move on," he said quietly. "Let's talk of other things. Ask me any questions and I will speak frankly."

What about religion? we asked. Is there freedom of religion as our Intourist guide had said?

"Why, yes," he said with surprise and pride. "In some churches you can see people at prayers. This is not a performance, but people who are actually praying. This is allowed.

"But I'm surprised you do not ask me about myself. I feel so unusual here in the city. I am stationed on the Chinese border, in a place where there are not many cars. It is hard to adjust to the Moscow traffic. I can tell you there are people in the north of China who live in true misery.

"But I would have to say, it is not from the Americans that we feel any real threat. It is the Chinese who are the danger. Americans are so sentimental."

Americans are so naive, we said.

Alex laughed again. "Not naive. Naive is not the word to use. Let us agree upon 'sentimental.'

"I can tell you that I like Americans. I have had several friendships with Americans, always very satisfactory.

"I have been in the American Embassy. I got drunk there with friends. To put it bluntly, I was carried out. But still, here I am. I am an officer in the Soviet army. I have a sensitive assignment. The stories about our police are exaggerated."

As he spoke, two soldiers marching side by side strode past us on the sidewalk. "They are on patrol," Alex said. "They are looking for soldiers who are gone without permission. This is often happening. When he is not fighting, the Soviet soldier is the worst in the world."

It was getting late. I have to go, I told him. I wished I had something of interest from America to give him, but my pockets were empty. Still, back at my hotel was an American magazine.

"A magazine?" asked Alex. "You would give me an American magazine? That would be wonderful. And I will bring you something, too."

We agreed to meet in two hours at a pedestrian underpass near my hotel.

Later, I would learn that several things—the fact that he wore civilian clothes, his border assignment, his open association with Americans—meant that it is likely Alex is an officer in the KGB. But at the time all I saw was a young man as curious about me as I was about him. A young man anxious to have any bit of news that had not been percolated through his monolithic government. I could see no harm in helping out.

So two hours later I walked through the shadows of the unlit parking area to the underpass. Alex was standing in the dark area beyond the steps. Apprehensively, I handed him my sack of contraband—*Time*, the *Stars and Stripes*, cigarettes, gum.

He handed a bag back to me. "My canteen," he said. "A souvenir of the Soviet army."

He hesitated a moment. "I have made some American friends,"

he said. "I wish there was a way—is there perhaps some way you could convey to my American acquaintances some words of friendship? Because I do feel friendship for them."

Maybe, I answered. There just may be a way I could do that.

The Mail

The mail situation here in Europe is putting a strain on my marriage. It used to be that when my husband came home I greeted him with a warm embrace, an announcement of the dinner menu, and a sympathetic ear.

Now it's a fast kiss, a mad lunge for his briefcase, and a quick dive into my favorite chair for a good read. Phooey on the old man. He can't possibly expect any attention when I haven't even had a peek at the day's letters.

I'd give anything if the mail came directly to our quarters, but the economics of the thing make that impossible. We have a German mailing address, but none of my pen pals is devoted enough to spring for double the postage for a note to me. And the telephone is definitely out, too. Those rates! These days the only way to "reach out and touch someone" is to mail them your fingertips.

You've got to understand that I am nuts about the mail. It's my passion. It doesn't matter if it's addressed to "Occupant" or "whom it may concern," or directly to me by name. If it came to me through the postal system I just can't wait to get my hands on it, rip it open, and devour it.

I've no real idea how I came by this mania, except that it does run in my family. After ten years of retirement my dad still ambushes the postman daily and snatches the goodies from his hand before they can be inserted in the mailbox. "I need to see the mail right away," Pop explains, "in case there's anything demanding an immediate response." Since bingo tournament announcements are about the most urgent items he's gotten in years, his enduring vigilance is definitely noteworthy.

There are a lot of swell things that come in the mail. First off, those letters from back home can really make your day. There's nothing like news of a divorce in the family or an old high school chum getting tossed in the slammer to really get me going.

Even talk of the weather can take the edge off homesickness, and if Mom throws in the word that that infuriating Mary Jane has finally gotten her comeuppance — well, it sets me up for the whole week.

Then there are the catalogs. I've put myself on mailing lists for catalogs of everything from designer clothes to tools to office supplies and birdseed. When a catalog comes I feel as if I've received a treasure. Not only can I look forward to hours of joyous mail-order shopping, but I also have the pleasure of knowing that if I order something, I'll get more mail.

I can't understand those people who write to Dear Abby about getting their names taken off junk mail lists. I like junk mail. On those days when no one from my massive file of correspondents has seen fit to write, I take heart from announcements from Columbia Record Co. and Spencer Gifts. Their pitch is always interesting, and it makes me feel good to know they think I'm somebody important, with a lot of money to spend.

My affection for the post carries over into my office life as well. I'm tight with Mike the mail clerk. It takes something major to keep me away from mail call at the office, but it has happened a couple of times. Mike understands me and has been known to bring the mail around to my section. Just to keep me from going bonkers.

Maybe if I'm good in this life, in my next one I will be a mail clerk. How glorious to be part of the chain of action that successfully sends a letter from Mom in Kalamazoo to son in Kaiserslautern. I can't imagine anything more gratifying.

In the meantime, I suffer through each evening waiting for hubby to trudge in with the day's deliveries. And that brings me back to the marital stress I mentioned earlier.

You see, my husband's been wondering: Have I always kissed the mailman so fervently?

Driving in Naples

Driving in a foreign country is always difficult. There are new rules to learn, new driving habits to absorb. But for those arriving in Naples for the first time the system seems incomprehensibly chaotic.

"This is not so," I was recently assured by Roberto Coperto,

Naples' Chief of the Driver's License and Carnival Ride Testing Authority.

"In Germany," Coperto explained, "Americans easily adjust to a different system. You learn that one always grants the right-of-way to the Mercedes. One understands that it is unsafe to travel on the autobahn at speeds of less than 100 mph. Everyone knows the striped crosswalk is a sacred zone of protection for the pedestrian.

"In Naples we also have rules and a philosophy of driving. It is only that they are different from what you may know."

"Do the differences cause problems for the American drivers?"

Coperto sighed. "Yes. Fainting is the worst."

I gulped. "Fainting?"

Coperto shook his head. "It is the cause of many accidents. It happens too often. The American driver, making his way through a tunnel on the expressway, on a bridge, or along an ancient road on the cliffside, is often so surprised to find a vehicle heading toward him in his single lane that he faints."

"Maybe if we understood the system better. Traffic lights for instance . . ."

Coperto snorted. "A good example. Americans do not understand that traffic lights are meant to control traffic. Why stop at a red light if yours is the only car to be seen? Why stop if there is not much traffic and you can easily make your way into the ongoing stream? Why stop if a lumbering truck approaches and you are a vigorous driver in a vigorous car? Why stop . . ."

"I see your point," I interrupted hurriedly. "But what about other traffic signals? What about signs? Say for one-way streets?"

Coperto shrugged in a vivid Neapolitan gesture. "It depends. It depends on the traffic, on the driver, on the importance of the destination. How can you call yourself a man if you let one small sign keep you away from the arms of the woman you love?"

"I think I'm catching on," I told Coperto. "It's a matter of face, isn't it?"

"Put it that way if you like. It is true one can accept the humiliation of being passed on the road only so many times. It is true that it is an insult when others forge ahead while you remain blocked. The Neapolitan driver makes use of every possible opening in the traffic. He must arrive at his destination as quickly as possible. He must not be insulted along the way."

"What about parking? I've noticed people park just about anywhere—sometimes even down the middle of a road. It snarls the
traffic horribly. Aren't there rules?"

Coperto looked uninterested. "Your question makes little sense.
If you want to park, you stop your car, you stop your engine, you
get out. What else is there to matter? If you wish to park, it is of no
concern to anyone but yourself."

"I've noticed the traffic doesn't bother pedestrians. They seem to
cross the street wherever they choose, without even looking for
oncoming traffic."

Coperto smiled patiently. "You think a man is safe on the street
because he stands on a marked crosswalk? In Italy this is not so. In
Naples every driver knows he must not strike the pedestrian. It
does not matter where the pedestrian stands on the street. He
must not be hit by a car. Since every driver knows this, why should
the pedestrian be concerned?"

"I've seen some pretty near misses."

"This is skill in driving."

"So, basically, you're saying that those of us in the American
community in Naples must simply rethink our philosophy of
driving. It's a bad mental attitude that causes us anguish and
accidents."

"That's true," said Coperto. "And the problem starts on your
own Navy base where departing drivers all see a large sign painted
on the ground that is totally contrary to the spirit of driving in
Naples."

"What does it say?"

"Yield."

Armed

Submachine guns. Automatic repeating rifles. Old-fashioned
carbines. You get used to seeing them around.

You get used to seeing them in particular places. On U.S. Army
bases in Germany soldiers march about with weapons strapped to
their backs. The guns become such a natural appendage that you
hardly notice them when troops stride purposefully by. You hardly
notice one dangling from someone's back as he buys a quick hot

lunch at the post snack bar. There are places where weapons are and aren't allowed, but you're hardly certain which is which. It seems like guns are everywhere.

Sometimes a civilian visitor might bring you up short. "Rifles!" such an innocent is likely to exclaim. "My god, are they loaded?" What are we supposed to do, you wonder, defend ourselves with insistent gestures? Anyway, it's only for training, so what's the big deal. You can walk away from your Army post and walk away from weapons.

Maybe. It depends on where you want to go. Take a trip to a lot of places and the first man you see as you deplane is the man who is there to shoot you if you don't act right. Coming off a luxury jet at Amman, Jordan, you see him standing there, eyeing you suspiciously. "I've come to see the Roman ruins," is what you want to tell him, but he wouldn't understand your words. "Be nice to these guys," says a knowledgeable passenger in a half-joking way. "Their clips are in."

And so they are. This is the way things are in the Middle East, you realize. Dangerous. Edgy. You wonder what would happen if a gust should sweep your hat away and you ran suddenly, chasing it down across the tarmac. Would they wait to see what you were doing?

Instead of dwelling on this question you concentrate on acting normally. You're actually glad, you tell yourself, this public airport is so well secured. That prevents bad things from happening to innocents like yourself. You're almost sure it does.

These days you're seeing the soldier with his compact, ugly weapon in more and more places. You see him in Italy, patrolling the airport corridors, standing outside banks, on the streets alongside major museums, randomly checking cars along the highway.

"*Buongiorno*," you greet him when he waves your car off to the side. Surely he is looking for a dangerous criminal and will at once realize this could not possibly be you. "Your documents?" he demands sternly. "This car is yours?"

What he is looking for you never divine. Maybe nothing particular. Whatever it may be, he is well prepared for the most dangerous eventuality.

You see him again in Turkey. He can be found in all the usual places but sometimes he is just walking along the street, monitoring the situation, ready to do what he must if it becomes necessary.

If you stay at a military hotel he is at the front gate, challenging you every time you enter. Your own weapons, the hotel registration forms state clearly, must be checked when you sign in.

The soldier you see in so many places could almost be the same man. He carries his weapon suspended from a strap wrapped round his neck. He keeps his finger on the trigger; the weapon's clip is always in. You get so you see him, and you don't see him. You are glad if he's there to protect you, but you wish he didn't have to be. Sometimes you look at him and then look quickly away, for he returns your glance with a bold, penetrating stare. No matter how natural, how pleasant you are, he never smiles. No matter how correct your actions, how filled with propriety, in case of any question you know his view is the only one which matters.

In the United States of America, we argue over the right and need for individuals to own handguns. The point is moot in many other places. Often the only recognized such need is for the soldier and his submachine gun, standing outside your bank, in your office entryway, patrolling the thoroughfare by your home. You'd think you'd never get used to that.

But you do. You get used to seeing weapons if you're on a military base a lot. Then you travel around and you see the men with submachine guns in many places. You get so that a soldier with his loaded weapon is an unremarkable thing, no matter where you come across him.

It's funny what you can get used to. It's funny and it's kind of scary, too.

Imagining Life without Dortmunder

I've been living in Germany for nearly two years and, to be truthful, my memories of what life is like in the U.S. are fading. But I hear stories.

I've heard, for instance, that you can't get a decent beer back home. There's no Dortmunder Union, no Rummel, no Schmucker's or Pfungstaedter beer. Over here, almost every town has its own brewery. In the U.S., I'm told, you can travel coast-to-coast, and wherever you go you see virtually the same beers—a couple dozen brands or so, and that's it.

Maybe the people back home don't much care about their beverages. I hear they drink their water right from the tap, instead of buying it in bottles like decent Europeans do. Over here we've got a choice between Hessen Quelle, Johannis, Apollinaris, Vichy, and Vittel, to name a few. I understand that in the States some people drink Perrier, but only on special occasions.

From what I hear there's no beer man in the States to deliver cases of beer and water to your house. In fact, from what I'm told, there isn't even a bread man to bring rolls by on Saturday mornings. Where the people in the U.S. get their fresh-baked *broetchen* I cannot guess.

Visitors tell me that in the U.S. almost all movies are in English and they're on the circuit about the same time the reviews hit the papers. Over here I keep a scrapbook of movie reviews, so that when a show comes to our post theater, nine months or a year later, I'll know whether or not I ought to go.

They say that TV back home is different, too. There are lots of channels to choose from, and all of them show advertisements for commercial products. They say that promotional messages for helicopters and rockets and other military hardware are quite a rarity, and you almost never see an ad urging people not to tell secrets at the *gasthaus*.

Those things are staples of our programming, and I can't imagine what TV would be like without them.

People tell me lots of little things around the house are different, too. All the appliances are 110 volts and so are all the plugs, so nobody uses transformers. And the door handles are almost always round, which must be very difficult. How do you open a round handle with your elbow when your arms are full of packages?

In the U.S., I hear, the windows all have screens. Such things don't exist in Europe, and I've gotten used to leaning out to see what's going on in the neighborhood. I'm not so sure I'd want a screen on my window anymore.

According to these same stories, when you shop at the Stateside PX, you're likely to get pennies back with your change. Over here, they round your purchase up or down to the nearest nickel. I don't think I've seen a penny since I've been in Germany.

My friends insist that a lot of military facilities back home were built after World War II. They're not just talking about shopping centers. They mean the whole works. They claim a lot of Stateside post gymnasiums were built to be gymnasiums and not converted from hangars. They know of military clubs that were not made from old stables and offices that never served as barracks.

If some of this sounds pretty amazing to you—well, it does to me, too. But these are the stories I've heard.

I'm not saying I believe them.

5

Getting Ahead and Getting Out

The Traumas of Possible Promotion

Effective Phrases

Have you heard of the U.S. Cavalry Catalog? It's a catalog consisting mostly of military items or military-related items. You can get stuff for your uniform there, like once when we couldn't find shoulderboards for the dress uniform anywhere, we finally ordered them from the U.S. Cavalry Catalog. I forget what they cost.

Now the catalog is offering something new. At least it's new to me. It's a book called *Effective Phrases for Performance Appraisals*. I was going to send off for the book and then tell you some of the phrases so you could do right by your people and maybe leave a short note listing the best ones on your rater's desk. But the book is too expensive. It costs $12.95 plus $4.95 for shipping and handling, according to the ad I saw.

I'd like to see you get promoted, but, to be honest, I didn't want to invest $17.90 on the project.

Anyway, this book is not the only one of its type around, and some of the others can be had for free. I know of at least one unit in Germany that had its own rather thick booklet of suggested phrases to be used in the writing of awards. As I recall, they liked "beyond the call of duty," "consistent diligence," "problem-solving capabilities," and "unflagging attention to critical details."

This book was very handy for the awards clerk because, no matter what the individual was being cited for, the clerk could easily find the most appropriate phrases. He found five or ten favorites and quickly discovered that just by juggling their order around he could create a variety of unique-sounding write-ups that all actually used the same words. Nifty.

Performance appraisals are a different matter, of course. They are more critical. Certainly in the case of officers, the OER is the piece of paper that determines if you get promoted or not. So you want it to say all the right things.

Unfortunately, what this means is that whoever writes the OER must be a person who isn't persnickety about telling the exact truth. The first thing the rater must do is make a general determination about the person he is rating.

Is the subject an OK officer who is able to operate a multiline telephone? Is he a nice enough fellow who sometimes brings donuts to the office? Does he recognize all the rank insignia, and does he always wear his uniform with the correct tie? Does he look sharp? Would he project the right image if he ever became Chief of Staff of the Army?

Or is he a dirty dog who should be drummed out of the service immediately? Is he the type of person who makes children cower and cute puppies whimper? Does he refuse to accept responsibility? Does he decline to laugh at Beetle Bailey?

There are specific phrases that must be used in each case. For the officer who is unlikely to cause a direct threat to the free world, even if he is promoted, the report must say, "Promote immediately! Promote ahead of his peers! General officer material! Possible chief of staff . . . ! Assign to senior service school! This officer's performance is unparalleled in every aspect!"

It's good if there are a lot of exclamation points.

For the person who got commissioned by accident while he was trying out for a role in *Police Academy III*, the report should say, "Excellent in staff situations. Top-notch administrative capabilities. Tremendous leadership potential. Not as overweight as he appears in photo."

It isn't true that everyone who gets promoted had perfectly written OERs. Some officers are promoted posthumously, after doing something brave in battle.

But now you don't need a book to tell you what to say when you're rating someone. Just copy from above, and you can be fairly certain of achieving the desired effect.

On the other hand, if you're the one who's about to be rated, it might be nice to give your rater a little gift that will cost you around $17.90. Chances are you can use all the effective phrases you can get.

Choosing Career Fields

If you're an officer who wants to get ahead in the Army, you have to be careful about the career field you get into. This principle applies to all the military services. If you're in the Air Force, you have to be a pilot, or else you can forget it. And in the Navy, if you're not the captain of a big boat, you might as well go on out in the garden and eat worms.

It is true that the Army gives you a broader range of opportunity. It used to be that command was what mattered, but recently the Army has gotten more into expertise. You can become a general just by knowing a lot about a little subject. These days, even computer people with unusual personalities are advancing remarkably. There's no doubt about it: The Army has changed.

But one thing that hasn't changed is that certain jobs remain the kiss of death careerwise. Don't let yourself get locked into one of these babies unless you're interested in trying to become the first 30-year captain since the Civil War.

Don't get roped in as the officer's club manager. Everyone despises this person. No matter how beautiful a Sunday brunch you put on, people will only remember the time the mayonnaise was off and a whole conference of colonels threw up. If you have Happy Hour, people worried about drunk driving will picket you. If you don't have Happy Hour, the post commander will be irate because he has nowhere to go after work but home. It doesn't matter that you did not set the actual policy. Everyone will blame the situation on you anyway.

Being an officer's club manager is a lot like being a writer. Anyone who knows how to eat knows enough to criticize everything you do. So give it up. Get into something else. If food is your thing, work with dining facility management. The people who eat in mess halls aren't allowed to complain.

Stay out of the minefield of Public Affairs. The complications are too great for any mere mortal to cope with. The problem is with perceptions. When you're the PAO, the public thinks your job is to make sure they get information. The CO thinks your job is to make sure the public doesn't get any information he hasn't personally approved.

What this means is that when the post garden club plants roses outside the headquarters building, your boss wants the picture on page one of the local newspaper. But when somebody miscalculates and lobs a mortar shell beyond the firing range and onto the grounds of an old people's home, the boss will be counting on you to keep the story out of the news.

The Public Affairs Officer often finds himself in the uncomfortable position of praying for a distant disaster. Most often he wishes for a small earthquake in a remote area of China where very few people live. He knows that such an event will take up just enough newspaper space to force the article about the general's daughter's latest escapade off the front page.

Be careful if you want to be a Foreign Area Officer. Here's a field that can take your career either way. Ten years ago the guys who picked Polish specialties got laughed at, but by now they're mostly wearing stars. Still, you want to be very careful. It's a safe bet that you shouldn't focus on Albania. You can't go there and neither can anybody else, and who would want to, anyway? It's unlikely that Albania is going to become a focus of world affairs anytime soon, but right now there's probably some specialist studying up on it like crazy. Do yourself a favor and pick another country.

Be careful about big countries as well. You don't want to be the FAO for Canada. Canada may be large, but it's right next door, they speak a lot of English there, and anyone can visit Canada whenever they want. So you're an expert on Canada? So what? All Americans are experts on Canada.

There are other fields of which to be equally wary. Like Organizational Effectiveness, because it so rarely is. And Chemical Weaponry, because the thought alone makes everyone shudder.

Petroleum Officer is no good, because the boss thinks all you're really doing is pumping gas.

When it comes to getting ahead in the Army, career field is the beginning and the end. Find a job that's indispensable, high visibility, and for which you have at least a moderate aptitude. Make sure it will always be possible to blame mistakes on the experts in some other, vaguely related field.

Stick with these principles and you'll be amazed at how quickly you can get ahead.

To Get Ahead, Be Important

Some people go about things all backward. They want to get ahead and get promoted so they'll become important. So they struggle along at mundane jobs hoping for some recognition. This strategy rarely works. The best way to get ahead is by being important. If you're important, you're sure to get promoted.

So who's important? Well, the person who's in charge of everything, but that's probably not you. Another important person is the officer who rides around in a special limo that's always got a police escort. Nobody knows what he does, but everybody knows he's significant.

That's the principle you've got to utilize. You may not be able to sign up an armed escort or arrange to have everybody stand when you enter a room, but there are some things you can do to enhance your image of importance. And if the illusion is successful, actuality won't be far behind.

1. Have a designated parking spot. The slot should be marked with your exact job title. Anyone else who parks there must be towed away. Parking up front in slots reserved for visitors or the handicapped doesn't count. A numerically reserved space doesn't count, unless you are number one. If you can't get the spot approved through channels, put a sign up yourself, preferably after dark.

2. Live in opulent quarters near the headquarters. If you can't get the main house by the HQ, the big one next to the "O" Club is an acceptable substitute. Barracks don't count, no matter how close in they are. If you have to choose between a house that's very near the headquarters, and one that has running water, take the

one near the headquarters. Your family will understand that it's necessary for you to be immediately available at all times.

3. Have your calendar published. See that your weekly schedule goes into general distribution and is posted at the PX, commissary, and movie theater. Make sure you have several appointments with very important people each week. Fill in the rest of the time with conferences at which you are the key speaker.

4. Have your lunch brought in. Arrange for a minion to serve you each day. Never go out to lunch, unless you are eating with someone who is very important, indeed. It is all right to eat at the "O" Club if they give you a private room.

5. Ask your secretary to put everyone on hold. Never pick up the phone until you know that you will not end up speaking to a clerk or secretary. Important people may speak directly to their own clerks and secretaries, but never those from other offices.

6. Go to the field in a camper. Important people do not sleep in tents, unless they are lined with Persian rugs. Take your own camper if you can't get one issued to you. Paint it in camouflage colors—going to the field in a camper is being important, but flaunting it is merely gauche.

7. Get a lot of work calls at home, especially when you have more senior visitors. These should be calls from people who need your quick decision or approval, or who merely recognize how vital it is to keep you in touch.

8. Have highbrow tastes. Important people tend to like things like plays, expensive wines, and thick books with no pictures or dialogue. Leave a few opera programs lying around on your desk.

9. Initial a lot of papers. This will lead people to think it's necessary for you to routinely review virtually everything. But beware, the key here is your tacit approval. If you are required to personally take action on these documents, your importance is diminished. Still, play it safe. Never miss an opportunity to initial any papers you see lying around.

10. Hold a newly created job. When you hold a job that's never been done, your OERs will be superlative since there is no basis for comparison. Good OERs aren't quite as significant to your advancement as your image of importance, but they don't hurt, either.

While the General Sits on the List

Waiting for promotion lists to be issued is not that big a deal. They come out every year, but the date is never the same. You see in the paper that yet another board has met. But you know it will be months before they reveal their decisions. You're used to that, and you've learned to take it like a soldier. Even when you know that board took a good look at your very own file, you're nonchalant. You find it easy to be low key.

That is, you do until the promotion list hits post. Because, for reasons that hardly make sense to mere mortals, the list is not immediately publicized. It goes into the general's office where he sits on it. And sits. He sits there until he gets the word that all over the world other generals are also sitting on this very same list. Only then, days or weeks later, is he allowed to announce the names of the chosen. And the sad likelihood is that the waiting has turned you into such a basket case you are no longer fit to serve.

But the situation isn't hopeless. There are ways you can help yourself. Here are some tips for passing the time while your local general sits on the list:

1. Take the general's secretary out to lunch. Tell her it's just a gesture of thanks for her overall helpfulness. Don't say a word about the list. Just have a pleasant lunch, watching her every move, evaluating the subtle nuances of her every remark. Does she seem bubbly and cheerful when you are around? Or does she make condescending remarks that seem to border on pity?

2. Ask the general. Ask him straight out if you're on the list. But be casual. Say "I'd sure like to know if my name is on the list you're sitting on, sir." He'll say "Yes, of course." But what does he mean? Does he mean, of course you want to know? Or does he mean, of course your name is on the list. Or could it be that he is worried about his golf game and never heard your comment in the first place, but is only making general conversation. Analyze his remarks from every possible angle, but don't ask him to clarify.

3. Take up smoking. Smoking is bad for your health, but what do you care? If you don't make the list you might as well die young. So practice the lighting up, the expressive gestures, the whole devil-may-care attitude that can be conveyed by a cigarette dangling sexily from your lower lip. If your name is on the list, it will be

easy to give up this nasty habit, and in the meantime it's a good way to keep you from chewing your fingernails down to the first knuckle.

4. Plan your retirement. Think about how great it will be if you don't make the list. Think of all the fun you can have living in Florida, going to the beach, fishing, having no responsibilities.

5. Take up a sensible exercise program. Work off your nervous energy by jogging. Add a mile for each day the general sits on the list. Try to go faster, as well as farther, every single day. Remember that being fit will help you to all the better carry out the new responsibilities you will assume when it's finally announced that your name is on the current list. And if your name isn't on the list, at least you'll be ready to gain a sense of achievement by running in a marathon.

6. Think positive. This is not thinking like ordinary thinking, but powerful positive thinking. Don't take the attitude that just because the list is out and the general is sitting on it, matters are completely out of your hands. Did you ever see the movie *The Shining*? Have you ever watched "That's Incredible" on TV? Or read *Ripley's Believe It or Not*? Weird things have happened in this world, many of them beyond logical explanation. Like, maybe your name really is on the list.

Paranoia with Good Reason

Do you ever find yourself wondering if maybe somebody up there in the hierarchy might just have it in for you? Like they're trying to send you a message you'd rather not receive?

Sometimes things happen and you can't help feeling that way.

Like when you drive to work and they won't let you on post because your sticker's expired. But wait, you tell the gate guard, this sticker's good until December. Look. It's written right here on the decal. December.

Then the guard gives you a funny look and says, yeah, but there's a whole new security program going on and everybody's been issued new stickers.

Everybody else knew about it. The word's out in messages and memos, on the radio and at roll call. And, the gate guard tells you, everybody else had the right sticker this morning. So what's your problem?

Ain't got one, you tell him, and park outside the gate.

Or how about when you go to work one morning, and you're wearing fatigues just like you do every other day, only everybody's all dressed up in Class As. They nearly faint when you walk in the door.

Special inspection today, they tell you, the general's visiting. The CO put out the word for everybody to wear Class As and for everything around the place to be made spruce. You can only grimace when you think about the haircut you meant to get on Monday and the tacky mess behind your desk you keep forgetting to clean up. And now you're in the wrong uniform to boot. And you can't figure out how that happened.

The CO can't figure it either. Take the morning off, he tells you, don't show back here 'til after lunch. Free time is always nice, but you know this morning you're not getting any prize.

Or did you ever come in to work and find some other guy was there in your place and doing your job? "Who're you?" you ask him, and he tells you he's the new man. What happened to the old one, you naturally want to know. Oh, they transferred him out or fired him or some emergency thing took him away, the new guy says. I'm not sure what it was, but it came up kind of sudden.

So you ask the first sergeant about it, or the CO, or whoever you can find who might have an answer. And they tell you everything's OK, it's been a mixup. These things happen. But look now, they say, this new man's got all his stuff arranged and cleared yours out and put it over there. Did you ever give any thought to whether you might like working in the motor pool?

A thing like that can make a person nervous about his status in the Army, not to mention in the world and life in general. But these things happen, don't they? Could it really be they're all by accident?

Did you ever have to wait a long time to get orders for your next assignment? You've got your PCS date all lined up and new people have been assigned to your quarters, and the new guy at work has been there a couple of weeks. And you know you're supposed to go, but nobody's told you where.

Finally the orders come and it turns out they're sending you to a post that's due to be closed down in a couple of months. Phased out forever, and you're only on your way.

So you call assignments and you tell them the trouble and they say, hey, if you've got a problem with that assignment we wish you'd brought it up a little earlier because it's too late to change anything now.

Did you ever have it happen that your paycheck didn't come? And you call the paycheck place and they explain how they're so sorry, they know it's their mistake, but the computer only lets them cut paychecks on certain dates, so now you'll have to wait until next month and then get two paychecks in one.

But then the rest of your mail stops showing up, too. And you wander on down to the APO to check it out, and you ask about mail, and you tell them your name. The clerk knows that name right away. He shows you the master locator book and there's a note by your name and it says "Addressee unknown." And no matter who you ask, there's nobody there who can tell you how *that* happened.

Did you ever get to feeling paranoid about these little incidents and worried maybe you've been working too hard, maybe things aren't actually so mixed up as they seem? Did you ever have just a fleeting thought that maybe somewhere, way up in the hierarchy, there's a fellow who's singled you out for special treatment like nobody else ever got?

Maybe it'll help to know and maybe it won't, but you shouldn't worry about those questions any more. Things *are* as mixed up as they seem and you're *not* the only one.

Wimpy Joe Is Your New CO

Sit down. Have a drink. You deserve it. It's happened to us all at one time or another, and we know just how you feel. You've just found out that your old pal, Wimpy Joe, is your new commander, and you're still in shock.

The name on the invitation to the change of command ceremony didn't even alert you. For one thing, Joe was not the kind of guy you'd ever imagined would be put in charge of anything. And for another, you haven't bothered to keep in close personal touch with him. You worked with him at one assignment years ago, and he's popped up occasionally since then. Every now and then you've heard stories about him, of course. The kind that begin: "Hey, remember Wimpy Joe? Well, wait until you hear this one. . . ."

When Wimpy Joe was a lieutenant, the story goes, he used to get dressed in his gym locker. It seems impossible, but anyone who'd ever seen Joe could easily imagine it. He was very thin, and shy to the point of being peculiar. But the real reason he dressed in the gym locker, the storytellers say, was so that no one would see the paisley boxer shorts his mother custom-made for him. Pantomimes of Wimpy Joe pulling on his shorts in the gym locker after PT were always popular at cocktail parties.

Your own experiences with Wimpy Joe made it easy to believe any of the stories you heard. He was the guy who organized the 4th of July ceremonies that were your community's annual show-case event. Under his expert coordination, parade time found the troops assembled on the green in front of the headquarters build-ing, while the brass and distinguished guests seated themselves in the local high school football stadium, five miles away.

Wimpy Joe always was considered a nice guy. He took the rib-bing well enough, and people always said his heart was in the right place. But he just wasn't an officer you took seriously. For a gour-met treat, it was said, he used to take his family out to the mess hall, where they served the food he loved best in all the world.

He considered dominoes good sport and wore a jogging suit whenever he played. His favorite movie of all time was known to be Walt Disney's *101 Dalmatians*.

There was nobody who claimed it was Joe's fault the Army didn't make a uniform that could properly fit his strange physique—he wasn't alone with that problem. But the tale was told that he was one of the few who actually had to change his branch because of his body. He wanted to be a chemical officer, but there's no gas mask in the world that could fit over *that* nose.

The problems didn't stop with Joe himself. Whenever he en-tered an office, accounts stopped matching up, training ceased to be effective, and the simplest missions went haywire. Even his family was affected. It was Joe's dog who, mistaking the general's wife for a member of his own species, pursued her amorously when she passed on her evening strolls. It was Joe's daughter who rollerskated out of control into the post swimming pool during a patio meeting of the Women's Evangelical Group.

Over the years you've heard news of Wimpy Joe; you've seen his name listed in assignment rosters. Joe has gone to Alaska, where you imagine him falling into a crevasse. Joe is now in Panama, where you suspect he makes the natives restless.

Over the years you've heard a lot of stories about Wimpy Joe, good for a lot of chuckles. That's why, when you go to the change of command ceremony and you suddenly realize that the person standing there at the rostrum is he, you feel more than a bit of shock. He's one grade and three career moves ahead of you, and you can't figure out how that happened.

Yes, old Wimpy Joe has been good for a joke for a long time.

But he's the one who's laughing now.

On Not Making the Cut

We just got a letter from an old friend. It was the first one we've had in a while, and I take that as a good sign. I take it to mean he's adjusting to his new life.

The old life took an unexpected turn a few years ago. In those days he was a jolly Army officer, a guy who liked the good times and the good guys.

In other words, he was just like a lot of single officers who are up and coming, who see the future as a broad path rolling out before them, and who are loving every minute of this life.

But sooner or later we all turn a little more serious. For him that change came when he met the right lady, married, and started a family. It all turned out to be just the thing for him; it was what he'd been missing before, maybe the emptiness that was behind all the drive to find those good times.

For a solid family man and an Army officer with a new sense of purpose life can look pretty good. There you are, entering your middle years, and the future is still rolling out before you, a path as broad and inviting as it ever was.

That's why, when it came, the blow was such a stunning one. He was like a million other majors, sweating out another list. But when this one came out his name was not on it.

The military is a funny kind of career. There are those crusty E-9s who make it to the pinnacle of their service and retire knowing they have achieved every possibility. But most people get out with the feeling there was just one thing more they'd like to have done: one grade, one command, one field of opportunity that wasn't open to them. Most people leave the military with the quiet knowledge there's a final cut they didn't make.

Of course we all put on the face of satisfaction. Talk to any battalion commander: He'll tell you his job is the pinnacle, he now feels satisfied that he's done what matters, and anything else is icing on the cake.

Now step over to the nearest promotion party, or the officer's club, or even the bowling alley. Sooner or later you'll hear someone talking about one of the generals, say a guy with two stars who didn't get his third and now has to get out. The way they say it sounds so cruel, and yet that's the way we think in this life. If you don't make the cut then it's time to go.

It's not really a dishonor to miss becoming a general . . . it's only a mild embarrassment. But when you're cut at the O-4 level, in a service with an O-5 selection rate of as high as 70 percent, you know what it's like to feel real pain.

Our friend felt the pain, and then he felt a disbelief. It had to be a mistake, a foul-up, something in his records that was not perfectly clear. He looked, and an advising officer helped him look, and they thought they found the problem: one report he hadn't maxed.

It took him about two years to finish fighting the thing, to collect letters from those who'd served with him at the time of the troublesome report, endorsements from current commanders, documentations, rebuttals, appeals, the whole complicated ball of wax.

But in the end the system didn't budge. There had been no mistake. He'd been good, but not good enough. There was no one clear reason. It was just that he didn't measure up — and that's the kind of news that hurts the most of all.

So he went to twenty and got out a couple of years ago. He's doing what a lot of people say they'd like to do: He's working in a stable job in one place with all the benefits and freedoms of civilian life.

He writes that the job is good and he's making a bundle of money. But if you read the message that isn't written you see the money hasn't changed the way he feels. He still feels the hurt.

It will never go away.

6

Heroes and Friends

A Hero

Big month, May. V-E and Memorial Day mean lots of talk about important events well worth remembering. In Europe the cemeteries one comes across in unexpected places and West Germany's barbed-wired eastern edge serve as reminders that our peaceful lives must not be taken for granted. From a Stateside perspective the events of the two Great Wars seem long ago and far away. Even those modern events that most closely skirt the edge of ultimate disaster—an Army officer shot while on duty, or a planeload of civilians downed for no reason at all—stun us only momentarily. It takes a surprisingly brief time for them to fade from our attention.

One thing about the big wars: They were full of events now familiar to us all. Even those of us born long after all the treaties were finally signed know something of the bridge at Remagen, the horrors of Verdun, the destruction of Monte Cassino. These stories have been immortalized, not only because of their military significance, but also because of the heroic acts they epitomize. The two world wars were full of heroes, bursting forth with them, in fact. It's a time we all admire from the long-range point of view, but along with the admiring I often hear a questioning as well. Do soldiers today have the same depth of courage? People can't help wondering. Will the heroes be there if we need them again?

The Army isn't in the business of training people to be heroes. It trains them to carry out difficult jobs well, no matter what the conditions. But sometimes the result of doing that basic thing is something that looks like heroism to an awful lot of folks.

Not long ago I opened the newspaper to see a photo and article about a friend of mine. He's a quiet kind of fellow, doesn't normally have a lot to say about himself. But I knew a few things. His wife was my roommate on a trip a few years ago, and one evening, chatting late into the night as roommates do, she told me a few things about her low-key husband and what he had done in Vietnam. He had saved a lot of lives, was what it all boiled down to. Saved lives by leading his men through dangerous places without regard for his own safety, by ignoring his own wounds to continue a critical attack.

The point of his wife's story was not to parade a prideful tale. More than fifteen years after these events, she confided, her husband looks back on them, not with satisfaction, but with a lingering question. Was there something more, he wonders, he could have done to help those who did not make it through? Fifteen years later he still mourns the loss of those men, and there is nothing even the most devoted wife can do to erase that sadness.

Except for that one long night's talk, we never discussed these matters. It was not until I read the newspaper story that I learned his actions had resulted in four Silver Stars and a Bronze Star. And I wasn't surprised to see his criticisms of some of the award citations. One, he said, was "not even close to accurate." He hadn't really done so much, he claimed. "There wasn't much bravery on my part. We just ran a good operation."

Running good operations is the very thing that heroes do. Especially heroes who live to tell their stories on those rare occasions when they feel so inclined.

The point of all this is that I'm proud to count such a person among my friends. And I wonder how many others there are, people whose friendship I enjoy but whose capacity for courageous sacrifice I have never realized. The more I think about it, the more I am certain there are many around me.

This month we reflect on important events long past; we think about brave soldiers and the incredible things they can accomplish. But we live in an unstable world, and our attention is also very much upon the present and the future. What if? We can't help asking ourselves. Do we really have the people to make the right decisions and do the difficult things?

We do. There is no doubt of it. This May, as we remember our past heroes, it would not be wrong to say a prayer for those to come, as well.

A Helper

Carolyn Todd knows almost exactly when the levee broke. It was just after 6 P.M. on Thursday evening, February 20. Just a few minutes earlier an official on TV had said there was nothing to worry about. It seemed to Carolyn the man had barely spoken those words when the news came that there was a 50-foot break in the levee, and the towns of Linda and Olivehurst had to be evacuated immediately.

Carolyn lives on Beale Air Force Base, which is near Linda and Olivehurst, which are near Yuba City, California. Yuba City became rather well known when a Rand McNally survey pronounced Pittsburgh the best place to live in America and Yuba City the worst. As a result, a lot of people drove up to Yuba City and its environs so they could see for themselves if it really seemed so bad. Until last week, it didn't.

When Carolyn heard the news of the levee break, she knew what to do. Many of the evacuees would be coming to Beale. She and her husband, who's first shirt of the hospital squadron, gathered themselves up and headed out. He went to the hospital and she went to the Recreation Center.

"Hundreds of people were already there," she says. "The initial group were in good shape—they were the younger ones who could get out fast. By 8:30 we were getting the ill and the elderly. That's when it got wild."

When Carolyn says "wild," she is talking about a busy time. As a volunteer with Red Cross disaster training, she helped with the nursing chores. This meant looking after terminal cancer patients, people on respirators, diabetics. One of the first people Carolyn assisted was an older woman in physical distress. "She'd gotten to the rec center with somebody who picked her up on the road. She knew nobody," Carolyn recalls. They put her in an ambulance and on the way to the base hospital, with Carolyn at her side, she suffered a heart attack. Happily, she survived.

While Carolyn spent the night assisting the ill evacuees, hundreds of other people at Beale were also helping however they could. Among them, Carolyn recalls, were Air Force people who'd been flooded themselves.

That night the waters in Linda rose to the rooftops. Of the 24,000 people evacuated, 6,700 found their way to Beale. There they were fed and housed, their health was looked after, they were assisted in finding family members from whom they had been separated, they were provided with donated clothing and other necessities.

"I'm amazed at the talent we had," says Carolyn. "We really pooled our resources and not on a planned thing. And it worked."

Carolyn spent fifty of the next sixty-four hours working the rec center, and during that time she saw all manner of things. "I'm not sure if this should be mentioned," she says delicately, "but I saw officers of high rank cleaning bathrooms and mopping floors. Everybody did everything."

She also saw the governor, a senator, and a congressman. But their brief visits left her unmoved. The image that stays with her is one of the blank faces of hundreds of evacuees as they sat in the rec center, listening to the news on a TV that carried no image. "The next morning when the pictures came on," she says, "that's when they broke down."

By Saturday the operation was so smooth that there was time to help reunite people with their pets and distribute food for those animals. By Sunday, the guests were gone—the lucky ones back to their homes, the others on to other evacuation centers.

They hadn't all been perfect company. Most were not exactly your landed gentry. Some had tried to wrangle extra medications, quite a number had come well armed, and a few had found mischief to get into on base.

But the vast majority were appreciative, and the time she worked left Carolyn with a different kind of feeling. "For years," she says, "as an Air Force wife I've seen the word 'pride' written on hangars and things. But I never knew what it really meant. Well, I do now, because that's what we've got here. We're proud of what we did at Beale."

Of course, the likes of Carolyn Todd are not likely to let it go at that. On Monday, February 24, the day before her birthday, she went into Olivehurst to see if she could help at the evacuation center there.

A Mother-To-Be

She's a soldier in this man's Army, and sometimes that's a hard row to hoe.

"I'll tell you how it happened to me," she volunteers. "I was TDY when I found out I was pregnant. So I called back here to talk to my first sergeant about it. When I came back to work they had taken up a collection for me. They collected from the whole company, from platoons where I don't even work. They tried to give me money to get an abortion. I told them just where they could put it."

The lack of privacy was a big blow. "When your test comes out positive they send the results right along to your commander. They don't necessarily even tell you they did it. They just send it right on to him, so he knows about it even before you've had a chance to really figure things out."

Some of them do get abortions. They save their money, or write home, or borrow from a friend in the unit. They go to Holland, or Switzerland, or some place they've heard about where you can go on a three-day pass and come back feeling like new. Ready to go back to work. Ready to be one of the guys again.

"It's lonesome, being pregnant," she says. "The other soldiers make you feel like an outcast. They take all the happiness out of it.

"I work in a good office. Before I got pregnant I'd say to the guys, 'Hey, here's what needs doing today. Let's get on it.' If I say that now, they all ignore me. They say 'You're pregnant, you can't do anything. Why should we?' It's crazy.

"People think I'd do this to my body for nine months just to 'get over.' But if you look at the roster you can figure out pretty quick

that there are a lot more males on sham time than females, pregnant or not.

"I got promoted just a little while ago. Now the attitude I get is:
'She doesn't deserve to be an E-5. She's pregnant.' It's like, no
respect, no rank. They took it all away. Even the CO is looking for
me to mess up, so I'll have to get out."

Somewhere in the not-too-distant past a man was in on the
beginning of all this. Now he's gone, and good riddance. "It's all on
the mother's part," she says. "If the father wants to participate he
will. But just because you're married, who's to say he'll be there
when you need him?"

Right now is a busy time for her. She's got to find out about new
entitlements, learn how to take care of a baby and herself, look for
an apartment, try to figure out how she'll manage the economics of
it all. And she goes to work every day, doing the same job she's
always done and standing at the edge of the PT formation when
the sergeant calls out for the profiles to step to the side.

"I want to stay in the Army," she says firmly. "I'll find a babysitter
who can come at a minute's notice. I'll get everything all arranged.
I know that I can do it. I understand my responsibilities."

She's met some other women in the same situation. They get
together and talk about things, and they've found out that they're
facing a lot of the same problems. They have hopes that before too
long they'll be experiencing some of the same joys, but they're not
deluding themselves about the realities.

"Sometimes we sit and cry together," she says. "It feels so good to
share. We all know that it's definitely gonna be hard. But you have
to make it."

Michele

What it's about, quite simply, is buying a doll for a kid named
Michele. With one L.

Michele is new to Army life and she's plunging into it full speed.
She lives on an Army base in Germany now, but before too long
she'll have to put up with all the stress and strain of a major move.
Early next year, before she's even had her first birthday, she'll be
coming back to the U.S. and she'll probably wind up living on a big

Army base here. When it comes to military life, Michele is going to learn it all real fast.

I wanted to get Michele a nice present. Partly to welcome her into military life and into life in general; partly because she's got a nice name.

So I went on a little shopping expedition, and I looked at a lot of cute baby things. There were outfits, but I didn't want to get her an outfit. I'm too smart for that, you see. I know that even the nicest babies sometimes throw up on their best outfits, and I knew that in later years, after Michele and I have developed a really close relationship, it would embarrass her to think she had once thrown up on the first gift I ever gave her.

I didn't want to get her a bib or blankets or crib sheets for the same sort of reason. Those are good practical gifts, but they aren't gifts that say "I love you." They aren't gifts you give when you're just starting a long relationship with an important new person.

The Teddy bears were tempting. I must have walked through miles of aisles of Teddy bears, fluffy and cute and begging to be cuddled. They were perched along with monkeys, unicorns, motherly geese and puppies—every one appealing for a baby to love it.

But none of them struck a chord with me. None seemed just right for Michele until, when I was on the verge of giving up, I came across the doll that was ideal. It was a perky Raggedy Ann. I've always liked Raggedy Ann. I like the fact that she's got a tradition. She's not just another sweet doll someone made up yesterday. And I like the fact that it says "I love you" right around her heart. With kids, I've learned, it's okay to send a forthright message.

I liked this Raggedy Ann, but she did have a difference. She was made with a dark skin, skin as rich and brown as my favorite chocolate.

I took her off the shelf, I looked at her closely, I turned to speak to the saleswoman. And then I froze, because the words I was about to say were not the right words at all. "Do you have a white doll like this?" was what I'd started to say, but the first syllable stopped just short of utterance. Suddenly all I could do was stand there, stupidly, with my jaw hanging open.

I was remembering certain moments when I had felt very smug. Once I met a couple who had started their own school so that their children would not have to attend public school where they might be instructed by black teachers. These were nice people, people considered upstanding and respectable, but I only felt appalled when I learned their views. I was disdainful of their archaic attitude, and shocked that it could even exist in 1985. But more than that, I felt superior.

Then there was the time I listened to a conversation about the high school dances. In some areas there's still debate over whether they should be "public" or "private"—read integrated or segregated. Such talk disgusted me. I found it hard to even pretend to be polite.

All of my life, from the time I was a small child, I've been around people of all races, all religions. I've had all kinds of friends, and I've always taken pride in that fact. Maybe that's the problem. Maybe somewhere along the line I started taking a little too much pride.

Because one day, shopping in a store not long ago, I somehow had the impulsive feeling that a black Raggedy Ann wasn't the right doll for the Michele who's just beginning life. For a moment, the thought formed in my head that I must ask the saleslady if this doll couldn't be had with white skin. Because white is my favorite color? Because I felt a white Raggedy Ann would somehow be a better Raggedy Ann?

I honestly don't know the real answer. But I did stop the words and I stood there for a moment, all my precious pride draining uneasily away.

"May I help you?" the saleslady asked at last.

"Yes," I said quickly. "I'd like this doll gift-wrapped, please." This sweet new Raggedy Ann, I had suddenly realized, could be just the thing to help the new Michele grow up to be a bigger person than her namesake ever was.

Mary Ellen

I am pleased to report that I have spoken to Mary Ellen and straightened out the misunderstanding about the chicken suit. From the picture Mary Ellen sent, I thought it was her husband, David, who was in the suit. It wasn't. It was Mary Ellen, all dressed up for David's birthday.

"Every year I do something more outrageous," she says modestly. Last year she dressed up in the chicken suit and went to the office where David, an Army lieutenant colonel, was meeting with two generals. She says he was surprised, but I wonder. After eighteen years of marriage to Mary Ellen, David is surely somewhat used to these things.

But I get ahead of the story. What I really wanted to discuss with Mary Ellen was her cats. She has twenty-two of them. "They're not pedigreed or anything," says Mary Ellen. "They're just a ragtag bunch of strays that adopted us and we adopted them."

They haven't always had twenty-two cats. Just a few years ago, for instance, they had only thirteen cats and one dog. They lived on a boat then, and the plan was that David would get orders to Panama and they would sail there. Only his orders got changed to Germany.

They took the cats (and dog) with them anyway.

Once there, they rented an apartment on the economy through a little deception in which David had no direct role. When the landlord asked "How many pets?" Mary Ellen answered "Three," thinking "Three" and "Thirteen" do sound rather alike in German.

Anyway, it all worked out. "We got our full damage deposit back when we left," says Mary Ellen. "We taught the cats to use the toilet, so there was no litter. David's only complaint was that he had to wait in line behind a Siamese."

Admittedly, that was one of the few times they have rented. "My house is as neat as anybody's, but I wouldn't want to rent to us," Mary Ellen allows.

Consequently, Mary Ellen and David have lived in some interesting places. They've lived in a floating house, a boat, a trailer, an elaborate mobile home and a $900 converted bus painted "Kermit green." "We have to live on the fringe," Mary Ellen explains, "because you can't get quarters with all these animals. The only thing we haven't lived in," she adds thoughtfully, "is a boxcar." One gets the feeling she's contemplating the possibility.

You don't have to talk to Mary Ellen for long, however, before you know that living on the fringe isn't strictly due to the animals. There's the chicken suit incident, for instance — not your average officer's wife's ploy. There's her job, which involves driving around in a pickup truck and selling yogurt. There's the fact that they'd like to augment their two pickups and mobile home with a some-what used Rolls Royce.

"I don't understand them," a general once told a new boss of David's, "but I like them."

"You couldn't really put us in a niche," says Mary Ellen. "When people know you're an O-5, they expect you to be a certain way. But they meet us and realize, in the case of David and Mary Ellen that's just not so. And maybe it's really all right."

Actually, there's proof it's all right. As Mary Ellen points out, "David's security clearance just went up, so I guess no one thinks we're a threat."

So, knowing all things are possible, Mary Ellen does enjoy the occasional fantasy. "If David ever became a general," she enthuses, "wouldn't it be great to live in a general's quarters and have a cat in every window?"

Well, maybe it would and maybe it wouldn't. But it's not a possi-bility the two of them are fretting over. They are too busy doing a wild and crazy thing—they are having fun, living life just the way they like it.

"Either David and I are incredibly dumb or incredibly smart," says Mary Ellen. "I just like to think we've found the secret to life."

I think they have found it, and I wish I could grasp it too. I have an idea it's really pretty simple—as simple as truly loving the ad-venture of moving to Germany with thirteen cats and a dog. As Mary Ellen puts it: "They all went. They all came back. It cost a lot of money. But we had a good time."

Somehow, they always do.

The First Sergeant

The first sergeant was on the phone.

"I'll be late," he said. "But I'll meet you for lunch. I've been up to my rear in alligators all morning."

The first sergeant's alligators are problems, and they range from the trivial to the truly troublesome. Soldiers who haven't cleaned up their rooms. Soldiers with marital problems. Soldiers with debts they cannot pay. Soldiers who are drunk, AWOL, in jail.

The first sergeant is their friend, counselor, disciplinarian, boss, enemy, leader, confidant. He's supposed to straighten these little matters out. He's supposed to slay the alligators.

Not that he's always been an angel himself.

"I was terrible," he admits. "It was immaturity. I was a draftee with an attitude and a ninth-grade education."

You can see by his record that he had some problems. Five Article 15s, all of them, he says, "for dumb stuff. I'd ask an NCO what would happen if I threw this rock through that window. 'Article 15,' he'd tell me. Crash.

"Maybe it was my way of saying, 'Hey, somebody, pay attention to me. Hey, somebody, care about me.'"

What changed him?

"I had good NCOs, I had a commander who cared, I had a platoon leader who was the best thing that ever happened to me. But I hated him then. I would have killed him for a dollar."

The first sergeant knows that some of his soldiers hate him now. It doesn't make him happy, but he believes in what he's doing and he knows sometimes there's a payoff that makes it all worthwhile.

"Once I had this eight-ball soldier nobody wanted. I gave him counseling statement after counseling statement. He wouldn't even read them, he'd just sign. He hated me then. It was hard while we were going through it. But we showed him we cared. In the end he came around. Ultimately he was one of the best soldiers in the unit."

Knowing how to talk to a soldier in trouble isn't something you learn in a class. You learn it slowly, over the years. You learn it because you've been there. You learn it because you care. The first sergeant has learned it in those ways and others. He's developed a strong philosophy.

"You have to know how to get a person's attention," he says. "Some people you have to holler at. You have to beat on the desk and yell. The opposite side is the person you talk quietly to and get results. You have to know these people before you can talk to them.

"Say a guy has an overdrawn bank account. You call him into the office to talk to him about it. You find out it's not his fault. There's always a reason, and he'll promise you that it will never happen again. But the minute he says, 'Uh,' here's what you do: You walk over to the door and you lock it. Then you sit him down and you talk. You support him by listening. You encourage him to go to places like ACS for help. You're caring, but you're stern."

If a tactical unit were a wheel, the first sergeant would be the hub. He's responsible for meeting the commander's requirements for meeting the mission. He's responsible for welfare. He's responsible for training. And more.

"When you're first sergeant," he says, "you're a role model whether you know it or not. You're a role model for the guy that will be in your job. Not next month or next year, but ten years from now. Every day soldiers are watching you and deciding if you are the kind of first sergeant they want to be.

"Then there's the new officer, the lieutenant. You train him, but you have to know how to do it without taking any authority away from that young officer.

"And the soldiers. You can expect to get telephone calls from them at all hours of the day and night. They'll call you up and say, 'First sergeant, the building is on fire. What shall I do?' You can't get mad. You tell him: Call the fire department. Next time he calls with the same question — then you can get mad.

"Or maybe they'll get drunk and call you. Alcohol gives a man false courage. By the time you get there he's sobered up, he's sorry he called, he says it was a mistake. But it's important to sit down and talk with him. You have to find out if there's a problem. When they call you, you have to go.

"I go to the unit at night to see what's going on. I leave the door open, I sit there in civilian clothes. You'd be surprised at who comes in and starts talking. Because if they hear you're OK, they'll come to you. They want somebody to talk to.

"Everybody has personal problems. Sometimes there's something that will push a man to the breaking point. When he does break, the first sergeant has got to be there. If he doesn't want to, then he needs another job.

"The most important thing is to have that soldier's confidence. Once you've lost that, then you've lost. Period."

An Army Bride

She's from Corning, New York. The place where they make the glass. "You ought to see the factory," she says. "It's really something."

The glassworks are something, but Corning is a small place. Europe is quite a contrast. Especially when you're 16 years old and a new bride and part of the Army family for the first time.

All things considered, she's doing mighty well.

"I'm used to doing things," she says. "But when I first got over here, I thought, it's so big and I don't even know what I'm going to do. One of the other wives took me around and showed me places to go and how to get around on my own. It really helped me."

Her husband is 19, an E-2, about to leave for a 90-day stint in the field. She isn't looking forward to his absence. "I don't know what I'm going to do with myself while he's gone," she says at first. But possibilities emerge. "I know how to ride the streetcar and the bus. I like to go downtown and just look around. It's so big." She was in her high school drama club and she may work on the community play. The more she thinks, the more things she thinks of.

"I went to one meeting about the field," she says. "They talked about how you would get his check and how to get the mail and stuff like that. I walk to the commissary and I take a taxi home. I get around."

She and her husband live in a little apartment right around the corner from the post. She knows he was lucky to find it. The station housing allowance he gets helps with the rent, but she wishes it were more. Still, money isn't a big problem.

"My husband is always saving," she says. "And I like that, because I know that I might not do it. He budgets. He gives me my money for the month and grocery money. And he budgets everything else.

"Right now, I wanted a car, but he said, 'Let's wait a little while.' He wants to wait until he gets Spec 4. From E-2 to PFC isn't the greatest raise."

She hasn't learned enough about the system to know what it is to be command-sponsored. "We haven't decided," she says in answer to the question. "Twenty years is a long time. But my husband likes the Army. He may want to stay in."

She likes the Army, too. But she knows she has a lot to learn. So far, everything looks so good. "When I came over here everyone was so different from where I grew up. They were really nice. They'd just come right out and talk to you. People in Corning keep more to themselves.

"We like the way people act toward us here. Friendly."

Sixteen years old, all her life up to now in Corning, and what she wants more than anything is to travel. "We went to Paris," she says. "It was nice. So big and busy. So many people, hurrying all over. We saw the Eiffel Tower. And we went to the museum with the Mona Lisa and all the other paintings they have there.

"Next, I want to go to Amsterdam. To see the flower show."

At first, she admits, her family wasn't too sure about the whole thing. "But my parents want me to be happy," she says. "I got married, truthfully, because I wanted to come over here, and I couldn't come, I couldn't be with him, unless we got married. Because it would have taken a lot longer for the government to approve my passport and stuff like that. I like it now that I'm over here. I really do."

That doesn't mean she never thinks about home. Sometimes, alone in her apartment in a foreign country, waiting for her husband to come home, she thinks about her sisters. Two are younger, one is older. "She's 18, she's going to college, she has her own car, she's really . . . sometimes I wish I was like that. But I'd rather be over here."

She's not sure just what her husband's job is. She's not too sure about how the Army is structured, or why we're in Germany or what the future holds. But she knows what she wants. She wants, one day, to be a housewife and mother.

"When we first started going out," she says, "he was just a boyfriend. I never thought I'd be married to him. But it's going good so far."

Name Dropping

My neighbor, Raianne, has been after me to mention her name in my column sometime. The reason I haven't done it is that it's such an unusual name. If her name were Mary, I could slip it in anytime and say, look, that's you. But with Raianne, I knew I'd have to explain that the name is pronounced as if it were spelled Ray-Ann. That's the kind of little detail that's important to a reader, but it can break up the flow of a good story.

Raianne has every right to have her name in this column. She's my best friend and has often turned up in tales presented here as a comrade-in-arms or major figure in some episode. Once, when writing about how I have to go to her house to use the phone, I said "she only gets irritated if I go over too often."

"Hmmmmm," Raianne said, "I didn't think it showed."

"Look," she added pensively, "I don't mind you writing these things about me, but why don't you put in my name, just once?"

It's a funny thing about using people's names in a column like this one. Some people really want you to and other folks will tell you any secret, if only you won't say where you got it. Teenagers, I've found, definitely want their names in, no matter how embarrassing their revelations. One young man on his way to basic told me all kinds of personal details and said he couldn't care less if I publicized the information with his name in bold letters at the top.

"Write me a letter about boot and your first impressions of the Army," I asked him, and he promised that he would.

Of course I never heard a word. That's because E-1s will not talk. They're all in shock, I guess; they don't even know what's in their own minds. E-2s have plenty of thoughts but it's hard to pry them loose. An E-2 will hardly tell you anything, unless he's repeating it from a manual. He's too scared of the repercussions in case he makes a mistake.

That's all over by the time they make E-3. A PFC knows what's happening and is perfectly willing to talk about it for full attribution. The trend continues so much that, to be frank, it can be hard to terminate an interview with a buck sergeant.

More senior NCOs turn cautious again. They are more accountable, and experienced enough to know the dangers of having your name appended to statements written down on paper.

There's a similar pattern for officers. Captains make the best interviews, unless they have to "check with their superiors." Captains who need permission to give an interview will never tell you anything that's really interesting. And colonels are a bore; they always want a promise they'll be able to read the story in advance and "correct" their quotes. That means, "Ye gads, that looks bad in print. I disremember saying it."

I get around a lot of problems by not mentioning people's names. Almost everyone I know in the military has an interesting story to tell, but a lot of folks don't want the attention that goes with putting it in print. And a lot of the stories, no matter how special, heartwarming, or absurd, have particular meaning to people in many different places. This isn't news you're reading here. These are opinions, stories, and inventions that have little to do with any one point in time or place. They're about all of us whenever they can be, so why pin them down with one particular name?

Raianne understands this as well as anyone, but she's a human person too. She's got a particular desire that's shared by a lot of generals and colonels and PFCs and all their wives as well. One time she'd like to see her name in the paper. Not for a birth or death or wedding announcement. And not attached to any statements that her boss is going to hold her responsible for, or that she will be asked to clarify later or supply additional supporting facts. It can't be anything her opponents could hold against her if she ever runs for election, and nothing that will make her mother say, "I told you not to talk to that reporter." No controversy, no debates, no stealing of another's limelight. Just a little notice to our readers that Raianne is here, and maybe a general observation that she's doing good.

Well, heck. Who am I to deny a friend a simple thing like that?

I've got this real nice neighbor. Her name's Raianne.

7

Rules and Regs and the Military Way

Smokeless

The war on smokers has gotten out of hand.

Not that I'm a fan of smoking—I'm not. I'm one of those who hasn't had an ashtray in the house in years. But the stringent antismoking steps the Army is taking still seem like too much to me. As of July 7, smoking and chewing tobacco will be prohibited in most Army-owned areas. And at Fort Jackson, South Carolina, troops are no longer allowed to smoke during basic training.

It's time to lighten up a little. I mean, if the Army is really so concerned about soldiers' health, why does it keep shipping them off to places where there are people who want to hurt them? Why does it send them crawling through minefields, encourage them to fly helicopters in the dark of night, and make them stay out in the cold even after their feet have gotten thoroughly wet? None of those things is healthy.

But I digress. The big problem here isn't a matter of health. It's a matter of image.

Run on over to your video store and check out all your favorite war movies. You know, *From Here to Eternity, The Great Escape, Dr. Strangelove,* and so on. Now watch them. What do you see? Soldiers. What are they doing? Smoking.

Why are they smoking? Because they are real men. This also, of course, applies to the women. I don't mean this in a derogatory way. Army women who smoke have learned all the tricks—how to light a match in a high wind, how to hold the cigarette cupped just so, how to rip it to shreds when it's all smoked up instead of merely crushing out the butt.

This is how people who are tough smoke. And who are the toughest people around? Soldiers. Take their cigarettes away and what do they look like? Wimps.

I would never insist that every soldier ought to smoke, or that any soldier should be smoking all the time. But you need a few smokers around to keep an appropriately macho image going.

There are practical reasons for smoking as well. If nobody smokes, how will the people in the trenches ever learn that three on a match is the max? If the ground isn't littered with butts, what trash will there be for recruits to pick up? If soldiers don't go around with cigarettes dangling from their lips, what will they do to look wickedly sexy?

This last is, of course, the real crux of the matter. It's great for soldiers to be fit and trim and eat lots of vegetables, but, hey, bank tellers do those things, too. Soldiers need to have a tough and dangerous air about them or they'll never get any respect. Until now, smoking has been just the perfect thing.

What we need to do is find some other activities that provide the same sort of reckless allure, in case smoking is completely banned. A few possibilities:

Cussing—Many soldiers already cuss, but few do it with real flair, and it is usually restricted to places where soldiers group together. Cussing in bars impresses no one. Perhaps the time has come to encourage cussing in other public places, such as libraries and airports. Cussing is not as good as smoking, but it does make an impression.

Spitting—Again, spitting is already done in some quarters. But few practice it with real skill. Spitting is a talent that can be developed. Accuracy and distance are qualities that everyone admires (isn't this really why we watch baseball?) and that are certainly consistent with the macho soldierly image.

More tattoos—There's a general impression around that the Navy and Marines have all the best tattoos. A few good Army tattoos could be just the thing. No little butterflies or "I love Susie." I mean tattoos of snakes that say "Tonight you die" and stuff like that. Manly tattoos, in other words.

I realize that none of these ideas quite does the job. Smoking was really the right thing. But even smoking doesn't convey a soldierly image if you have to sneak around to do it.

At this rate, Army folks will have to adopt a new mascot: Rodney Dangerfield.

Missouri Punch

By now you've probably heard the good news. The USS *Missouri* got its silver service back. As it was, I'd been living in fear of getting invited to some shipboard soirée. How could I possibly attend if there was a chance they'd try to force me to drink out of a paper cup?

Happily, the whole thing has been worked out. It was just a misunderstanding. The state of Missouri had been keeping the silver for the USS *Missouri*, and they temporarily forgot that they might have to give it back one day. It's easy to see why they'd want to keep it. The silver service consists of a silver punch bowl, 321 goblets and some other stuff that all adds up to an estimated value of $250,000.

The set was donated to the original ship, *Missouri*, by the state of Missouri in 1904. The current USS *Missouri*, which I guess should actually be called the USS *Missouri* II, was decommissioned in 1955, and at that time the silver was "loaned" back to the state.

The USS *Missouri* was recently recommissioned and based in San Francisco, a city where accoutrements count. When the captain of the ship said he wanted the silver back, the governor of the state said it ought to stay in Missouri, right handy in the governor's mansion in fact. His logic was that the stuff was never really given to the USS *Missouri* (II), but to the original *Missouri* ship, which has evidently gone to that great good beyond where expired vessels repose.

It's a relief that the matter has been resolved. The issues were always clear. Who needs the silver more? The governor of a state that is located kind of in the middle of our very large country? Or the captain of an important vessel that is based off America's most cultured city?

You've got to ask yourself, how many people who are important enough to require silver goblets for their beverages have ever visited Missouri (the state)? In my opinion, the people of the "show me" state are just looking for something else to show off. Admittedly, show-offable items are probably hard to come by in Missouri. But there must be something.

The USS *Missouri* should have the silver. A lot of important people are sure to be visiting the ship, now that it's so handily located, and they've got to be entertained properly. Imagine, for instance, if you were the Korean Consul and you were invited to lunch on the *Missouri,* and they served your drink in an old peanut butter jar. How would you feel? You'd feel like the U.S. Navy was a cheapskate organization, wouldn't you? You'd wonder if a 40-year-old ship without proper tableware is really capable of defending your interests.

But what if your drink came in a silver goblet? You'd be cheered, right? You'd feel confident that the U.S. has all the resources necessary to keep the world safe and free. Your goodwill would likely spill right over to Missouri (the state). You'd consider buying a condo in St. Joseph.

Obviously, the real issue here goes beyond a minor dispute between the *Missouri* that is moored in the San Francisco Bay and the Missouri that is moored in the plains. The real question is, what about our other ships? What have the people on them been eating off of?

What I'd like to do is make some kind of an inventory of silver punch sets. I want to be sure there are enough to go around and that appropriate personnel have been designated to keep them polished.

The thing about life on a ship is that you never know who's going to drop in. We're not just talking local VIPs, like the mayor of Haifa or the Bahamanian governor. It's not unusual for the real biggies to show up. Think of all the times you've seen Bob Hope on ships with a bevy of celebs in tow. Think of all the times our own president has visited ships to see if they're really as big as they look on TV.

Now ask yourself: How embarrassed would you feel if it turned out all these people had to drink out of ordinary glasses instead of sterling silver goblets?

That's exactly what I thought.

Greensleeves

Ever since word got out that at least one general has told his troops to roll up their BDU sleeves "whichever darn way is easiest," military policymakers have been in an uproar. With the entire Army clearly divided into two camps — cam in versus cam out — the pressure is on to establish a servicewide policy. But as the controversy rises, most top brass view the BDU cuff question as one best kept at arm's length.

"This kind of decisive leadership is what makes today's Army great," a DA spokesperson told a press conference that was held not long after the local sleeve-ease ruling was announced. "We encourage this kind of practical thinking among commanders, as long as it doesn't get out of hand. After all, we don't want our soldiers to start rolling up their pants legs or anything dumb like that."

Until the unofficial statement of support was made public, other high-ranking officers remained wary of comment. "I'm unavailable for interviews," one commander told all callers, "unless it's off the record. Unless it turns out that my statements coincide with the Pentagon view, which is likely to be cockeyed."

The reasons for the officer's reluctance to go on record were all too clear to those accustomed to following military procedural practices. "A lot of us got burned on the umbrella issue," fumed a Pentagon long-timer. "We went after those umbrellas with all the firepower we had, and look what happened. We got labeled wimps. I want it on the books that we were never advocating floral designs. We were advocating dry. I know when to come in from the rain, but some people don't. They need umbrellas."

Others have viewed the BDU sleeve decision in a different way. "It's a purely face-saving device," said a promotable brigadier who does not now command, or ever expect to command, the Army's

25th Division in Hawaii. "The fact is that BDU sleeves are shrinking as much as ever. Who can roll them up with the camouflage out and get the right effect? There's not even enough fabric in those cuffs to go around a nerd's biceps. Letting soldiers roll their own in their own way is the only way."

In the field, the decision has proven popular. "I like rolling up my sleeves like this," said Spec 4 Rusty Tumble of the 1st/42nd Engineers as he demonstrated. "See, I roll up the cuff and then roll and roll and roll and that's it. Three rolls and I'm good to go. We used to have to cam out and it was really hard to get each sleeve even unless you were a general and you had an aide to help you."

Also in the field, more junior commanders are wondering if Pentagon support for the sleeve-ease situation gives them a new leeway.

"I'd like to make a decision that would maybe be real popular and get picked up by the whole Army eventually," said one lieutenant who thinks recent developments may provide him with a chance to stand out and possibly get a better job. "It could be something real simple, like encouraging troops to carry nose rags in our unit colors. You know? Or maybe we could let them wear just one piece of shiny brass with the BDUs. You know? Wouldn't that look sharp?"

But for every soldier who is pleased by the sleeve-ease cam in look, there are others who think the cam out roll should be mandated by an official ruling. "BDUs are for camouflage," explained one patient NCO. "If soldiers are allowed to roll the sleeve up willy-nilly the cuff ruins the camouflage effect. That's dumb." When it was pointed out to the NCO that the arms that extend out from rolled sleeves also break camouflage the NCO commented, "Not much I can do about that, now is there?"

All in all, the controversy over sleeve rollup reveals the problems that can arise when policies are not clearly set forth in Army Regulations. "I've been wearing those Jim Palmer colored bikini-type shorts under my BDUs," revealed one soldier. "So far, nobody's complained."

The Form

Here's a true story:
I once got a new form approved and printed.

To those of you who don't work in the bureaucracy that may not sound like much of an achievement. But anybody who's ever worked for Uncle Sam can appreciate the significance of my feat.

Some people brag about fast times in marathons. Others are proud of the money they've earned, the high scores they've achieved on tests, the number of hearts they've conquered.

Everybody is proud of some outstanding accomplishment.

Mine is the new form that I got approved and printed.

It was tough.

First, I had to find out how to go about it. Nobody official knew.

I had to do research in the MOS library, where I read regulations, amendments to regulations, supplements to regulations, DA pamphlets, brochures, booklets, and clarifications.

These documents tell you it is possible to invent a new form. They tell you how big it has to be, what it can and cannot say, whether or not it should have borders, and what you have to do to get it approved.

They tell you that you have to talk to the Forms Control Officer.

Nobody likes to admit he is the Forms Control Officer, but if you ask him straight out he'll usually own up. Forms control is extra duty that is always assigned to the most unlikely person. Usually it's the dentist, the vet, or the CO's driver.

Ask around. Sooner or later you'll find him.

In order to get a new form approved, you have to get a form number.

In order to get a form number, you have to have a copy of the form. But you can only get a copy of the form from the printer, who will make a dummy of the form. But he will not make a dummy unless he has a contract. And you cannot get a contract unless you have a number, which means the form has already been approved.

So you have to be creative.

You have to fill out four copies of a Form Request form, asking for approval of your new form.

Nobody ever has any Form Request forms.

So what you do is find one in an old sample book and copy it on the copy machine when no one is looking, because it's not allowed to copy forms unless they are all filled in and you cannot fill in the Form Request form in the sample book or everyone will see what you are up to.

Then you take the form and your Form Request forms and a smelly cheese sandwich over to the legal office, because the rough draft of your invented form must be legally approved.

If you sit in the office with your smelly sandwich someone will quickly see you and sign your Form Requests right away if you will only promise to leave.

Now it's back to the Forms Control Officer for a form number. You will have to leave all your paperwork with that person for about a month. At the end of that time you need to start calling every day to find out what's going on. Eventually they will tell you there has been a complete staff turnover and everything is lost and you must start all over.

While you're waiting on that you should start calling the Government Printing Place and find out how to get an Exception to Policy. You want an Exception to Policy so you can get your form printed anywhere but at the Government Printing Place.

It's not that their work isn't good. It's just that it's slow. Extremely slow.

You get the information on how to get an Exception by being friendly to people at the Government Printing Place over the phone. You must never, never tell them the reason for your call. Just dial and say, "Hi, how's tricks?" and hope they will let something slip about the procedures for getting an Exception to Policy. The topic is bound to come up.

Once you get your Exception, you can get a contract and take a duplicate of your invented form to the printer and bring a dummy back to Forms Control and get a number, and take it back to the printer and pretty soon you will have your wonderful new forms.

If you're reasonably quick, you can get all this done in one year. I'm proud to say it took me just 10 months. (And then I left that job. The form I invented has never been used.)

An Instructive Offer

Unless it's quickly nipped in the bud, a new brouhaha over wasteful military spending is about to erupt. The *New York Times* has revealed that the Pentagon has been paying its suppliers from $500 to $1,200 per page for the training manuals that accompany weapon systems. At those rates the total charges quickly swirl into the millions, leaving taxpayers and budget officers alike in a state of perpetual gasp.

But not to worry. There's a way out of this situation. There's a way to acquire these all-important teaching tools at a mere fraction of their present cost. It's a way that is simple, easy to implement, and makes sense in every way.

I will write the training manuals.

Right away you can see the savings will be enormous. I am willing to do the job for a mere $300 per page. Knock $100 million off the Defense budget right there. The $300 figure applies, of course, to instructional manuals dealing with the fundamentals. How you start up the tank, where the gas goes, how to steer, how to make the turret swivel, and stuff like that.

To be honest—and I want to be up-front about this in every way, right from the beginning—I would have to charge more for certain more technical directions. When you get into target acquisition, putting the helicopter down in a crosswind, and anything having to do with trajectories or outer space, we're looking at $375, maybe $400 a page.

It's still a bargain if I do the job.

Right now you're asking yourself about qualifications. "Sure, she's cheap," you're saying, "but can she write directions down in a clear way?"

Yes, I can. Just so there's no doubt, here's a short sample of my instructional writing:

To Open Door

1. Grasp door knob firmly. Turn knob to the right.

1a. For those in European theater, grasp door lever, press down. Lever may also be depressed with elbow, knee, or loaded grocery bag.

2. Still holding knob or lever firmly, push inward with a firm motion.

3. If door does not move, pull door outward with a firm motion.

4. If door does not move, jiggle knob or lever, and try push-pull motion. Push-pull. Push-pull. This is a test for stuckness.

5. If door does not move, knock with a solid rapping motion.

6. If no one answers, seek out your supervisor and request a key.

As you can see, the above directions are clear, concise, and to the point. That is how all training manuals would be if I were given the job of writing them.

Another point is that the above directions are completely accurate. The Defense Department has been terribly upset with the frequent errors in present manuals. It's important to get the details right when you're telling people how to arm nuclear warheads or send up death ray satellites. If the details aren't right, serious problems can arise.

One thing I can promise you for sure: If I were writing the training manuals I wouldn't include a lot of dumb mistakes.

Well and good, you're no doubt thinking, but what about the volume of work? Could I possibly keep up with the job?

Let me assure you that I could.

First of all, I am a quick study. I was in an M-1 tank once and I still remember exactly how to shoot down a thermos of coffee: Look through the viewer, find the hot object, center it up, push the white button. Bam. That's about it.

I figure I could turn out four pages of instructions per hour. That's about as fast as I can type accurately and, as I mentioned earlier, I'm well aware that accuracy is all-important in this job.

So, I don't want to belabor the point, but this is something you might want to keep in mind. Think about the fact that the military spent around $400 million on training manuals in 1982, and a lot of those had to be done over because of mistakes. Think about all the new weapons systems coming up and the terrible budget crunch that's going on. Think about these things, but don't worry, because there is a way out, a way to save big bucks and get the job done right at the same time.

Let me write the training manuals. I can start most any time.

Exceptional Ability

I was discussing awards with the battalion awards specialist, Snood. It turns out the system doesn't work the way I thought it did.

"What are most of the awards given for?" I asked him.

"Leaving."

"Leaving?"

"Roger. Leaving the unit is one of the most intelligent career decisions a soldier can make. There's not a more appropriate occasion on which to recognize a soldier's initiative than the day before he leaves. So we give a lot of awards out then."

"What kind of awards do you give people who are leaving?"

"They're certificates," said Snood. "We fill them out with the specific information that relates uniquely to the particular soldier who is receiving the award. It's a highly personal recognition of achievement."

"What kinds of things do you say on the certificates?"

Snood drew a thick sheaf of papers out of his briefcase. "We draw on this reference file of appropriate comments," he said. "For example, here you see listed 'sound judgment,' 'professional competence,' and 'keen analytical mind.' These are all important attributes. Naturally they may vary. For instance, sometimes we find a soldier has exhibited 'keen judgment,' 'a professional analytical mind,' and 'sound competence.'

"On the other hand, we might say . . ."

"I think I get your drift," I interrupted hurriedly. "What are some of the other things for which awards are awarded?"

Snood consulted his papers. "It's all pretty basic," he confessed. "You know. Exhibiting initiative. Comprehensive knowledge in application and implementation of policies and procedures."

"Whoa," I interrupted again. "Give me a specific example of that last one. What would a guy do to get an award along those lines?"

"Implementation of complex policies?" Snood smiled. "That's an easy one. We give it out all the time. Say you get your uniform on right every day for a month. That's worth an award if you learn the right way to roll up your BDU sleeves, but usually you have to have your insignia pinned on correctly as well. We have high standards."

"There's an award for wearing the right uniform?"

Snood nodded. "Yes, and it's real cute, too. It looks like a little bow tie."

"What else do you give awards for?"

Snood consulted his list. "Demonstration of exceptional ability is a good one. We give a lot of awards for that."

"What does 'exceptional ability' mean?"

"It means he was able to read the SQT manual."

"And then do well on the test?"

"Not necessarily. Usually if he passed the SQT it counts for 'outstanding exceptional ability.'"

"I see. What are some other ways to get awards?"

" 'Tenacity of purpose' is a biggie. That would be given only in a case where a soldier showed up for work almost every single day. 'Devotion to duty' also is worth a certificate. That's a case where he showed up for work in uniform almost every day. And we give a certificate for 'completing the mission with commendable results,' which means he didn't get an Article 15.

"A very important award is given in a case where 'all facets of his operations received consistently enthusiastic comments by inspecting officers.' "

"Does that mean he passed the IG?"

Snood looked uncomfortable. "Not exactly. Passing the IG earns a 'rare and exceptional certificate of honor.' The 'consistently enthusiastic comments' is awarded to anyone who receives any unsolicited praise."

"From who?"

"Anybody."

"I get the gist of what you're telling me, Snood," I said. "But there's one thing I'm curious about. What if a soldier came along who was truly outstanding, who did the job better than it had ever been done before, and who brought real glory to the whole unit through his topnotch performance?"

Snood looked confused. "I don't know," he said. "I don't think there's an award for that."

How Assignments Are Made

I ran into Capt. Crumb the other day for the first time in a long time. He's working in a personnel shop now and he wanted to know how come I never write anything about how assignments are made.

"That's easy," I told him. "Everybody already knows all that."

"Oh, yeah?" he said defensively.

"Sure. It's common knowledge that each soldier's record includes a dart with his name on it. When it's time to be reassigned, somebody in personnel puts on a blindfold and tosses the darts at a big board listing all the possibilities. Presto: You're on your way to Korea. It works that way for everybody except the folks actually working in personnel."

"What do you think happens to them?"

"They all assign themselves to Hawaii."

Crumb looked disgusted. "It makes me darn mad to hear stories like that," he said. "The truth is, the dartboard system has been out for months. It's a whole new Army these days. We've recognized that soldiers are human beings too, and we're taking that into consideration in the assignments section. We've developed a whole new concept in assignments."

I was skeptical. "Tell me about it," I said.

"To start with," Crumb told me proudly, "we're actually reviewing the dream sheets before making new assignments."

"You're kidding."

"No. It's true. But it is a problem. We're finding that we just don't have that many openings in Tahiti or Paris. Everybody wants to go to Fort Ord, but nobody wants Hanau, Germany."

"So what do you do?"

"We come as close as we can. Say someone wants Berlin, but there are no vacancies. We send them to Fort Sheridan, Illinois."

"I don't get the connection."

"Fort Sheridan is near a big city with lots of nightlife and it's right on a lake so you get that island kind of feeling. It's a lot like Berlin."

"I see. What you're saying is that if someone wants Florida, but you couldn't swing that, you might send them along to Naples, because Italy is also a peninsula?"

Crumb made a note. "Good point," he said. "That's just the type of correlation we're looking for. We're making every effort to meet the service member's desires."

"What about the available jobs? How are you doing with matching up mission requirements and the soldier's MOS?"

"That's another area where flexibility is important," said Crumb. "And we're finding most soldiers agree that variety is the spice of life."

"What are you talking about?"

"Take a skilled cook. What is cooking but a form of chemistry? A mess sergeant makes an ideal medical technician if that's what's needed. It works out great. A lot of those guys just love to give shots."

"I don't think this sounds so good."

"You just don't understand how in-depth our assignment analysis is. Say a man's records show he can't take the heat."

"You send him to Alaska?"

"Right. Or else to Ford Hood, so he can learn how to cope with his problem. Or say a guy speaks fluent German."

"Wait a minute. I know what's coming. You send him to Izmir?"

Crumb beamed. "You're catching on. We figure Turkish should be a snap for anybody smart enough to learn German."

"Well, Crumb, I can see your job isn't easy. Now that you're looking at so many factors so closely you must find it's often very difficult to match a soldier with the right assignment. Tell the truth—do you still pull out the old dartboard when that happens?"

Crumb looked aghast. "No way," he asserted, "those days are gone forever."

"So what do you do in a tough case?"

"We spin a bottle."

8

Generally Speaking

A General Drag

If you're thinking of becoming a general, you probably ought to think it over some more. There's a lot more to it than you may realize.

Most people think it would really be great to be a general. They think about riding around in a big car and having a driver and getting to wear that leather belt. They think about pistols and prestige and being first in line at buffet dinners. But there's more to it than that.

Take those buffet dinners. When you're a general, you get invited to a lot of them. After a while, mashed potatoes and steamship round don't look so good, even if you are first in line.

A lot of times the parties that generals go to are not fun parties. They are official parties—that means if you get invited you have to go, even if you're pretty sure nobody you like is going to be there.

On the other hand, when you're a general, even if you do get invited to fun parties the real fun doesn't start until you leave. Everybody wants you to come, so they'll know their party is important, and then they want you to leave, so they can let the good times roll.

When you're a general, people are watching you all the time. If you go to a ceremony, you have to know just which music means stand up and which music means sit down. Everybody else will do exactly what you do. If you are wrong nobody will tell you, but later they will laugh about it during a coffee break.

When you are a general, people don't like to tell you about your little mistakes, but they do like to tell everybody else. If you get spinach in your teeth at the luncheon, no one will mention it. Later, when you get home, you'll wonder how long the spinach was there. Was it there when the TV newsman interviewed you? Was it there when you congratulated the officers' wives on their garden club project? Was it there when the general with two stars more than you stopped by unexpectedly? Everybody knows except you.

Generals can never be late for work. They must always arrive precisely on time, or earlier. This is what makes the Army work. The mechanic is on time, because he must sign the car over to the driver. The staff is on time, because they want the general to see how hard they are working. The staff's staff is on time, because they want to be like everybody else. When you are the general, you cannot be flexible about getting to work.

Generals do not call in sick. Even if they have a very bad headache or can barely stand the thought of another day at the same old job, generals have to show up. The only excuses accepted from generals are being in a coma or under anesthesia.

Generals must always be prepared to make remarks. These remarks must always be praiseful, upbeat, inspiring, and energetically positive. They must be made before ladies' auxiliaries, Boy Scouts, troop units, neighborhood gatherings, and international meetings, and at sports events. The purpose of the general's remarks is to speak well of what those gathered are doing and make them feel good they are doing it. It doesn't matter what it is.

Generals have their pictures taken all the time. This is because there are so many generals and they pass through their assignments so quickly that nobody can remember what they look like. Constant photographing helps keep the community alert to just who the general is. The general is the guy with the photographer running after him.

Nobody ever develops any of these pictures.

The bottom line is this: There's a lot more to being a general than a big office and your own secretary. So next time somebody asks you if you want to be one, don't just leap at the opportunity. Think it over very carefully first.

The Main Man at JCS

Vessey is out. Crowe is in. That's the way it goes with the military's superjobs. Just as soon as you get a feel for exactly how unwilling one guy is to confront the issues, they come along and give the job to somebody else.

Of course the world is anxious to know everything possible about the new man, and ever since the announcement was made I've been waiting for the telephone to ring. But nothing has happened. So either my phone is out of order, or else the media has somehow overlooked one of its best possible sources on the new JCS Chairman: me.

I know Admiral Crowe. I am well aware of the precise pronunciation of his last name (rhymes with "ow!"). I have had a chance to observe him in social and work situations, and while our actual direct dealings have been limited (we shook hands in a receiving line), they have been adequate to allow me to make some cogent observations about this man who now holds our nation's top military job.

First, it can be said without fear of contradiction that Admiral Crowe is a tall man. He is not so tall as to invite parody or questions concerning his hormonal balance, but he is certainly taller than average. He is, in other words, adequately tall, without the onus of being excessively tall.

This tallness, I feel, is a quality that will stand him in good stead in his new role. It will provide him with an opportunity to look down on those who are shorter than he is, yet still, on occasion, maintain a proper perspective by gazing up at those who are taller. This, I think, is a good thing.

Additionally, Admiral Crowe is what might traditionally be described as a "fine figure of a man." He seems to have achieved a level of personal fitness that is entirely appropriate for his age, grade, and current position. That is to say, he is fit enough to avoid the ignominy of nicknames such as "Blimpo," "Fatstuff," or "Big Boy," yet not so fit that people will worry he might be out jogging over the lunch hour, rather than devoting himself to making important decisions.

Our new Chairman also has a decided ability to deliver the *mot juste* when it is called for and has even been known to indulge in the *bon mot*. These little French habits are entirely apt in an individual who will be facing questions of international import, as well as all-too-literal impact.

I remember so well the early days of our acquaintanceship. Once, when I had just arrived at his home for a little gathering of several hundred intimates, he greeted me at the door with typical cordiality. "Good evening," he said, as I recall. "Welcome," he continued, with the unforced tact that comes so naturally to all great statesmen. "Come in and someone will get you a drink."

Then there was the occasion of the Admiral's change of command, as he departed the NATO headquarters in Naples. On that day his knowledge and skills were abundantly evident. Throughout the complex ceremony he was constantly aware of precisely when to sit and when to stand. When called upon to make remarks, he was fully prepared and spoke briefly, but not too briefly, on a topic that, if memory serves, had something to do with the NATO headquarters in Naples. The subject could not have been more apt.

It should also be noted that on this and all other occasions when I personally observed the Admiral, his uniforms were absolutely clean. His carefully developed grooming habits are an important plus in his new, high visibility role, particularly when you consider that this is a man who often wears white.

Crowe does not approach his new job alone. His wife, Shirley, will be there to support him. Of course I also know her quite well, having often seen her as she sat at the head table at our wives' club luncheons.

While the Admiral is clearly the right man at the right time, it is true his selection does have drawbacks. Primarily, there is the fact that he is in the Navy. However, it can be said to his credit that he has never denied this fact, never attempted to conceal it or deceive anyone concerning his affiliation. He has apparently convinced the right people that he is able to put aside his unnatural predilection for the marine, and that his admittedly aquatic perspective will not dampen his overall efforts as JCS chairman.

On the whole I can say, based on my own personal contact and up-close observation, that Admiral Crowe is unquestionably a four-star admiral, and thus meets all requirements for his new job.

I wish him well.

General Housing

How many square feet does a general need? This is the latest question to raise the ire of congressional watchdogs. Senator William Proxmire, especially, is up in arms over the idea that senior military officials may soon be living in something that almost approaches comfort.

The project that has attracted the most attention is a $3 million building plan for Fort Hood, Texas. New homes for three generals and seventeen colonels are scheduled to be constructed there.

It used to be that generals were allowed only 2,100 feet to live in. The new houses will grow to 3,000 feet each. The official reason is that the generals need more room for entertaining. But critics aren't buying that one. After all, 200 of the new square feet are being put into bedroom space. Proxmire wonders what kind of entertaining the generals are planning to do.

This is the most irritating kind of thinking, illustrating, as it does, how few people understand the special demands of military life.

Of course the generals and colonels need more space for entertaining. The reason is, they're too embarrassed to take their friends to the Officer's Club, and the NCO Club won't let them in. Senator Proxmire says the building money should go to a more worthy project, but I imagine he's thinking of a weapons system or the computerization of another something.

If he would propose putting the money into officer's clubs, I'd go along with him. Barring that, new officer housing looks like a good idea. At least, I'd rather drink cocktails at somebody's new quarters than almost any officer's club I can think of.

Senator Proxmire also criticizes the new houses because they will have both fireplaces and heating systems. He thinks the duplication is excessive, for people who live in the middle of Texas. But that just shows he doesn't understand generals. Generals are naturally cold-blooded people. Otherwise they wouldn't be generals, they'd all still be lieutenants. It's simply not their fault that they need extra heating. Personally, I'm all in favor of spending a few tax dollars on a fireplace for a general's home. I'm in favor of spending tax dollars on almost anything that a general might find heartwarming.

Then there's the fact that generals tend to be tall—thus the call for extra bedroom space. I suppose there may be a few short BGs around, but your basic general is usually over 6 feet tall. He needs a king-sized bed to sleep in and a lot of dressers and cabinets for all his military paraphernalia. His wife probably has some clothes as well. There's no way they can put all that stuff away in a bedroom that's 8 x 10.

So when the specs say the new quarters will have 200 extra square feet of bedroom space, I'm certain they're mainly talking about closets. No matter how you look at it, there's no such thing as too many closets.

And let's not forget the matter of interservice rivalry. The way things stand now, admirals just love to invite generals to their quarters for the sheer fun of embarrassing them to bits. Most admirals live in marvelously big old houses with lots of charm. At an admiral's party, you'll always find a lot of helpful people in cute uniforms serving drinks.

Most generals live in small, unattractive quarters. If they want help at the party they have to pay their drivers extra to serve the hors d'oeuvres, which your usual driver will only do if it isn't bowling night.

Who can blame these poor officers for feeling mortified?

Not only that, but people who are stationed at Fort Hood, Texas, have special needs. Fort Hood is sixty miles southwest of Waco. In other words, it's nowhere. People who live in such a setting deserve a little something extra.

I admit, there are some points about the new houses I don't understand. The description I read said they'll have covered carriage entrances that cost $6,000 each. It's been a long time since I've seen a general pull up in a carriage, but then I haven't been to Texas lately.

I don't object to better housing for the brass. The way I see it, once the generals and the colonels get their new quarters, they'll probably be disposed to see that everybody else gets nicer housing, too. At least, that's the way it would work out in the best of all possible armies.

I'm just hoping that's the one we've actually got.

Ten Tips to Stardom

You've been in the Army awhile. You want to get ahead. You want to become a general so you can (a) be powerful, (b) make more money, and (c) tell certain people to go jump in the lake. But becoming a general officer does not happen automatically. It takes careful planning, starting right now.

Here is how you do it:

1. *Have the right jobs.* It doesn't matter how terrific you are if you're always in charge of typewriter maintenance. For career progression, you've got to have jobs that are powerful and/or glamorous. You need to have important jobs in important commands. If you're not the absolute decisionmaker on issues of presidential concern, you should at least be an adviser to someone who is. Or, an adviser to the adviser's adviser.

It doesn't matter how you actually do at these jobs, only that you held them. If getting fired gets you high visibility, it can actually be a help in the long run.

2. *Become an expert.* Command used to be It, but these days being an expert in an esoteric field is just about as good. Find a subject area no one in the whole Army knows anything about. Become completely knowledgeable in this field. Point out to the top brass that there is a crying need for experts in your area. You are headed for the stars.

Promising fields of expertise include South American tribal languages, cultural development in ancient Sumeria, tactical spear warfare in the Sudan, and anything having to do with hygiene in the desert.

3. *Have the right photo.* The photograph in your file must be perfect. Your uniform and physique must be perfect. Your expression must be perfect. You must look serious, but not icy. You must appear authoritative, but flexible. Your expression must convey

128 ★ *Polishing Up the Brass*

your warmth as a human being, your capabilities as a service member, and the image of a person who, while outstanding in every way, poses no competitive threat to his superiors.

Practice this expression in front of your mirror for several minutes each day during the week before your picture is taken. Do not allow anyone to observe you.

4. *Have the right friends.* Your friends should be upwardly mobile, but not so glorious that you appear wimpish in their shadow. Be kind to losers, but do not hang around with them excessively.

5. *Have a lovely wife.* Your wife should be subtly attractive, but not stunning. She should dress in tasteful, tailored clothes appropriate for her age. She should be loyal to you, active in community activities, and thoroughly knowledgeable on matters of military etiquette. She should smile a lot and have a sympathetic attitude.

Do not allow her to wear your rank until you have actually pinned it on.

6. *Keep the right hours.* Be at work when your boss arrives. Be at work when your boss departs. Do not worry about becoming excessively fatigued—no one cares what you do in between arriving and departing.

7. *Have excellent taste.* You don't have to have much, but what you do have should be very nice. Do not wear double-knit suits off duty. Do not wear plaid golf pants unless you are golfing. Do not drink any wine that costs less than $2 per bottle (liter, not gallon). Do not serve canned soup to guests. Do not make furniture by covering cardboard boxes with old tablecloths. Do not wallpaper your bathroom with beer labels.

8. *Be a gracious host.* Act as if you actually like the people you invite to your home. Provide them with plenty of food and drink. Listen to their conversation in an interested manner and keep your own remarks brief. Do not go to bed before the guests have left.

9. *Have nice promotion parties.* Every time you get a promotion, even before you are a general, throw yourself a swell party. Let everyone see what a fine fellow you are, and be reminded how appropriate it is that you are getting ahead.

Do not send out party invitations until the promotion list has been released.

10. *Know someone on the selection board.* Be married to the

sister of a board member. Be the former XO of two board members. Live next door to the board chairman.

Always keep your dog off his lawn.

General Entertaining

Sooner or later you're going to have to square your shoulders and face the question. You've been putting it off, because deep in your heart you already know what the answer must be. In the core of your social soul you know that it's time.

It's time to have the General over.

Sure you're worried, but you shouldn't be. As with anything else, advance planning and preparation are the key to the success of this operation. So sit down, relax, and mull over these few basic questions. Consider your options and alternatives. Just a little thought will go a long way toward avoiding a major disaster.

1. Will the General be comfortable in your home? Things will go much better if the General is at ease. Do you have a nice soft easy chair with a commanding view of the party room? This is where the General should be seated. Naturally you will also need chairs for your other guests as well. Folding metal ones will do.

Or, you can help the General feel at home by encouraging him to stand with his back against the wall. Be sure the area is free of protruding pointy objects. It's nice to have a sturdy mantle for him to lean on, and a hanging mirror so he may unobtrusively check to see that his tie has not slipped.

2. What will you feed the General? Avoid awkward, greasy foods, such as fried chicken legs or grilled ribs; breakable, drippy foods, such as thin potato chips with heavy dip; and feminine, rabbity foods, such as carrot sticks or unstuffed celery.

Feed the General something he can eat like a man and that will not stain the front of his shirt. For a casual evening, feed him pigs n' blankets with mustard dip. For a more elegant affair, feed him pigs n' blankets with a Dijon wine-based mustard dip.

3. What will you say to the General? It's a good idea to plan your conversational gambits in advance. It's all right, for instance, to ask the General about his vacation, but he probably won't be riveted by a lengthy description of yours. You're also safe in seeking his

opinion of the region in which you are located, the probable outcome of the football season, or the likelihood that a new Army uniform will be introduced shortly.

Avoid official and/or controversial subjects, such as the results of the last IG, the probability that your leave request will be granted, the presidential elections, and the Miss America Pageant.

4. Who will talk to the General's wife? Remember that not all generals' wives are the same. Some generals' wives are most comfortable in conversation with other generals' wives, but there are many who also enjoy an informal chat with community volunteers, unwed mothers, church officials, interior decorators, and the sergeant who bakes those fancy cakes for official functions. Invite a cross-section of these types to your little gathering, and you'll have all the bases covered.

5. How will you keep the General amused? Food, drink, and your own effervescent personality are all a help, but they will not do the job alone. The General is used to ceaseless activity and a constant demand for his opinion. Ask yourself if this is the kind of man who is likely to know that Donald Duck's nephews are named Huey, Dewey, and Louie? If he is, then a game of Trivial Pursuit is in order. If, however, you're fairly certain that this fine man is a bit low on brights, you could try another party game. A good one is to blindfold one person who must then guess everyone else's identity by feeling their thighs.

If the general is cool to games, consider showing a noncontroversial videotape, such as *Patton* or *The Big Red One*.

6. What should you do in case of emergency? Your excellent planning makes this unlikely, but the unexpected can happen. What if war is declared, one of the guests turns out to be a closet conscientious objector, or the General mistakes the bowl of Velvet Hammers for a fruit punch?

These situations require an expert's assistance. Just open your front door and call for the General's aide — he's sitting out front in the car that's blocking your driveway.

Bruce

Have you ever noticed how a person's perspective changes when they get to be buddies with the brass?

I mention this because my friend Bruce recently got a star. The minute I heard the news I started seeing things with a new view. Bruce's ascension will mark the first time I've been pals with a general, and I'm finding it puts a different spin on things.

Let me say right away that I don't mean to offend any of you other generals who've thought we were such good friends all these years. You are all nice people. But Bruce has really been a buddy.

One time, for instance, he escorted me and my tall friend, Mary, to a jumping night spot. Once we got there I somehow wound up dancing with a person who was probably the shortest adult male on the European continent. I felt pretty silly until Bruce started showing off his best steps with tall Mary towering over him. Seeing another couple who looked just as dumb as my tiny partner and I did make me feel a lot better about the situation.

But that's the way it is when Bruce is around. He just naturally puts people at their ease.

That's partly because he's such a casual and open kind of guy. I remember a party he once threw. It was to celebrate a birthday and a successful surgical procedure. The operation was of a delicate and private nature, and so we all enjoyed talking about it in great detail. Everyone brought appropriate gifts. Ours was an intimate garment, which I won't describe in detail, but I will say that Bruce accepted it with tremendous grace.

For awhile, my husband and I lived near Bruce, which was handy. It meant we could easily tell when he was making party preparations, and we didn't have to wait for the formality of an invitation. Another of our neighbors was a Nigerian man who later overthrew his government and is now in jail.

These are the kinds of shared experiences and memories that have made us feel so close.

As far as Bruce's qualifications for generalship, I can't say enough. I know he is an extremely neat person, and I'm sure that is an important quality for a general to have. His quarters are always very tidy. Like, if you dropped by, you'd be able to tell somebody lived there, but you'd figure they must be expecting their mother-in-law to show up at any moment.

Generals have to go to a lot of parties, and Bruce will be very skilled at that. He is a sociable person, especially if he happens to be drinking a beer and eating some chili and talking about Texas.

(Although if you're thinking of starting in with the Aggie stories, it's wise to remember that while Bruce likes to tell them, he doesn't always like to hear them.)

Another thing about Bruce is that he looks very well in a large office. Sitting behind a big desk, with a flag or two behind him and an attractive secretary out front, he cuts quite an impressive figure. He looks . . . respectable. Which is, in fact, precisely the way you'd want a general to look.

But from my point of view, the most interesting part about Bruce and the star isn't Bruce at all. It's how the whole thing makes me feel. Last month I was just a regular person with a bunch of nice, but regular friends. This month, thanks to Bruce getting promoted, I'm pals with a general. And it's a fact that the vision of Bruce wearing stars has brightened my entire outlook.

Now I know anything is possible.

9

Choir Robes and Combat Boots

Moments on the Serious Side

Choir Robes and Combat Boots

Choir robes and combat boots. Something about that combination is what finally made her cry. There were other things that made her throat feel tight. The helmet, a stark green contrast against the white cloths on the altar. The wail of a baby, reverberating mournfully through the church. The empty pew, where the widow would have been seated, had she felt up to coming. These things made the woman's head feel strange, but there were no tears.

She hadn't really known this soldier. She'd met him once or twice and that was it. To be honest, she could never have picked him out of a crowd. She came to the service only because it was the right thing to do. She came as a token of the respect every person is due.

She left with some different feelings.

Because during the service she started thinking back over the years, back through all the times the phone had rung in the night.

It was always for her husband and she could tell, just by the voice of the caller, what kind of message it was. She could hear a grim professionalism that told her this was no alert, this was no news of a break-in or minor accident.

Time after time she had handed the receiver over to her husband, heard his voice turn stark, watched as he quickly dressed and left the house, or lay in bed awake, eyes staring at nothing on the ceiling.

Once or twice things had taken a turn for the better. A swimmer, lost in the currents for hours and presumed long drowned, was found treading water in the final stages of fatigue. But that was an exception.

Usually the calls came when there was no more doubt. A car wreck. A brutal murder. An equipment failure. A freak accident that should never have happened.

The frequency of the calls varied only with the husband's job. Sometimes they came often — every weekend or even more. Sometimes a few months went by without the black news penetrating into her protected world. Over the years she became almost used to them. She ceased to be shocked.

"That's awful," she'd say, and then turn back to her book or the TV or roll over and fall asleep. What else to do?

Once, at an outing with civilian friends, she'd surprised herself. The men were executives, much more highly paid than her military man. Their wives were well groomed, beautifully dressed. They talked about layoffs and interest rates and plummeting production. "It's serious," one of the men said grimly.

"Serious?" she heard herself saying. "I'll tell you what's serious. At our house when the telephone rings on evenings and weekends it's as likely as not to be somebody calling my husband to say there's been a death. It's always a possibility in the military. It's always serious business."

They'd stared at her for a moment, and she felt abashed. Where had those words come from?

Now, today, sitting in the church, she almost wished she'd said something more. But it was probably just as well.

Sitting through this service for a man she'd hardly known she felt peculiar. The preacher, it was clear, hadn't known the soldier very well either. He made appropriate remarks about the fruits of our labors, and the contributions each of us makes and for which we will be remembered. They were fine statements, but they didn't really touch the woman.

The congregation sang a hymn, said to have been one of the soldier's favorites. It was a hard melody to follow and the voices wavered and the woman felt no part of what was happening.

Even when a friend of the soldier's, straining to keep his voice even, stood to read a few verses from the Bible, the woman was somber, but controlled.

She probably couldn't explain what it was that reached her. All she knew was that when the small choir stood to sing she felt a sadness inside her grow as large as the church itself. And she thought about all the phone calls over the years, and all the memorial services and the helmets resting on altars. And she noticed one of the singers was wearing immaculate white robes over a soldier's BDUs and polished black boots.

And she stared at her lap and she wept.

Captain Lorence

In California this week the name of Paul F. Lorence is much in the news. Capt. Lorence was the weapons-system officer of the F-111 that did not return from the bombing raid to Libya. Capt. Lorence and his pilot, Capt. Fernando L. Ribas-Dominicci, will not be back.

Lorence was from the San Francisco Bay Area. He still has family there, and this connection has provided our area media with a news director's dream—a local hook on events of global significance. Thus, we have seen countless interviews with Lorence's mother, Bernice, and his stepfather, Richard Kruger. We have heard innumerable times that Lorence was a dedicated officer who was well aware of the risks his work entailed. We have watched the family, tearful and proud, come to terms with a son's untimely fate in the discomfiting public glare.

Along the way we have learned that many members of Lorence's family were fliers, that Lorence himself learned to fly when he was 16, that he once played in an ROTC Band, that he graduated at the top of his navigation training class at Mather Air Force Base, and that he used to live in the Lido Terrace Apartments in Rancho Cordova, California.

It's the job of newspeople to ferret out such details, to make the story whole, yet some people are offended by this kind of treatment, by what they perceive as an intrusion into the Lorence life at a time when it might be best to keep a respectful distance.

But this kind of coverage has a solid purpose: It makes people understand what we did in Libya was real.

California is a long way from Africa. To most Californians — to most Americans — the antics of a half-mad Middle Eastern dictator are something that provoke an irritation barely strong enough to last through the morning coffee. To Californians, until now, the security checks at an airport have been mainly an annoyance that usually seemed half a joke.

And, serious as it is, a bombing raid on a distant land has a dreamlike kind of quality. We know it's real, and yet . . . it doesn't seem much different from other news we see on TV. We know terrorism has become a terrible problem, and yet . . . how does it affect us here? We fume all through the cocktail hour and fret about cancelled vacations. Then it's off to see the latest movie or spend some money at the shopping mall.

Underneath it all, we know we have no worries. Our boys in uniform will take care of things. And we're certainly safe so long as we stay at home.

These are cushioned attitudes, and for most Americans they are reality. Most Americans have not lived overseas, have not lived in housing areas guarded by soldiers in full battle dress, have not seen the effects of a terrorist bomb on a headquarters building or a commissary.

The TV has also been full of interviews with military people who are overseas. Most seem concerned, but at the same time they have taken a courageous stand. They will not let their lives be ruled by terrorists, they will not spend a tour in hiding, they will take precautions but they refuse to live in fear.

From California it is easy to admire these positions and hard to understand them. There is no way to really appreciate what it means to deal with fear when there is no fear at hand.

But there are some things we can understand. There's Paul F. Lorence. He lived here and now he's dead. That brings it all right home.

Most Americans are supportive of the air strikes against Libya.

Most are proud of the way they were effectively carried out. That's how Bernice and Richard Kruger feel, in spite of their own personal loss.

It's particularly reassuring to know they hold that view. Because, out here in California, they are among the few who know what it all can really mean.

Independence Day

Fourth of July and you're farther than far from home.

It's hard to live away. It's hard to be far from family and friends, for instance, when a birthday rolls around. But usually a new friend will help you count the candles, admire a gift you've bought yourself, or drink a toast to your health.

It's hard to be far from family and friends at Christmas. You wonder if they got your gifts, if the color was right, if your mother was surprised. But you can walk the streets of London or Rome, Kaiserslautern or Crete, and see the signs of Christmas celebration so familiar. You can share the spirit. You can drink it in wherever you are.

Fourth of July is different. It's our national birthday, the beginning of what we are. It's baseball and hot dogs and marching bands. It's apple pie and Mom and everything we've grown up with. It's American pride.

Wouldn't it be good to be home for the Fourth of July? Wouldn't Dad just smile, and cousins and aunts all laugh and tell a million stories of everything that's happened this whole year? And the weather would be so nice there'd be a picnic outside in the yard. Old friends would come and you could sit and talk and tell about the things that have been going on, tell about the problems and decisions that face you. Maybe even straighten out a few things in your own mind. Old friends don't have all the answers, but they make fine listeners.

Maybe your hometown would have a parade, with your sister the drum majorette as the big star. And everybody would stay up late and watch the fireworks, and drink a few beers, and sit in the yard talking in the dark and listening to the crickets until the smallest hours of the morning.

Wouldn't it be good?

If you could be home for the Fourth of July, you'd have a time. You could make a weekend of it, take the kids up fishing, camp right along the stream bank. Or visit one of those really big amusement parks, with a roller coaster that whirls you upside down. Or look around a famous city like Boston, or Philadelphia or Washington, D.C., where you could take in the history of it all.

And wherever you went you'd see other people doing similar things, having a good time, enjoying their American holiday. Every one of them would know just what it was all about. For at least that one weekend, and especially that one day, every one of them would be thinking something about being an American and being glad.

It's not like that when you're far away.

Sure, there are plenty of other Americans right where you are. Probably they've got things planned for the day, things that will be fun. You can go and grill some hot dogs, maybe listen to a band play. It'll all be OK. It'll all be fine.

But not like being home.

Because when you leave your friends to head back to your quarters you can see that you are not at home. You can see that you are in a foreign place, and you cannot help but feel alone and unfamiliar. More than ever, you wish that right now you could be home. More than ever, you wish that at least today for just one day, you could be back in the real world.

Being here feels like a sacrifice.

If it is, it's a sacrifice with a kind of honor to it. If it is, it's a sacrifice for the sake of the folks back home. You're here so they can march in those parades and fire a million dazzling fireworks into the sky, all across our nation, all on one celebratory evening.

Those fireworks mean you have done your job.

So you stay far, far from home, watching the edges of freedom, and doing things that are sometimes so meaningless you could cry. Next year, or the year after, you'll be home for the Fourth of July. You know that as you know that the sun will rise in the morning. You know it because it is the fruit of your labor.

There's a trick question that asks: Is there a Fourth of July in Europe? And the answer is yes, there is, just as there is a 2nd of May or a 21st of October.

But the trick is on the jokester, because the fact is, there *is* something special here at that time. Something special here for you, brought by you, shared by you. You're an American, and it's with you wherever you go.

There's a Fourth of July wherever you are. You and the rest of the world can be sure of it.

Living Insecurely

It is pitch dark out. I am making my way through the grounds of a luxury apartment complex to an overlook where I will take in the magnificent nighttime view of Lake Geneva and the beautifully lit city curving around its shore.

The sight is breathtaking, but my mind is on something else. While my husband and the friends we are visiting relax with after-dinner conversation, I have, without pretense of stealth, clambered my way to the overlook. The house behind me, I know, has just been sold for something around $2 million. The front of the apartment complex is protected by an imposing wrought iron gate and TV camera system. But back here there is only a waist-high wall to block off the grounds of these exclusive residences.

I, the unknown visitor, have made my way through yards and gardens to enjoy the city view. No one has challenged me. There is no evidence of real security measures.

I find this strange.

Scene: I am in my own neighborhood, taking a final evening walk with the dog. Fall is here and I have bundled up against the chill — hat pulled low, bulky jacket. I make a final circle on a bit of grassy parkland not far from the General's house.

There is a small guard shack there. As I approach, two soldiers step out quickly. They are dressed in BDUs, their rifles are slung over their shoulders. "Hello," I call out as I see them.

I pause for a moment, we chat. The weather, the duty, the dog.

I go into the house without giving the incident another thought.

Scene: Two men have called on my boss. They are German. They say they are doing a security study on *kasernes* throughout our Corps. It is contract work, so they carry no U.S. identification.

The boss is new, just in from the States. He talks with the men at length. But a coworker is concerned.

She telephones and learns that our headquarters does not know who the men are. She reports their license plate number to the MPs and the German police.

She becomes more worried and places more calls. At last, she finds the office that has sent the men. They are exactly what they say they are.

I am glad she has checked them out.

Scene: I am driving onto an air base with a carload of friends. We all flash our ID cards, as usual, but the AP asks me to remove mine from my wallet so she can examine it more closely. I am curious, but not annoyed. Why was I singled out?

One of my companions gives me a long look. "Early 30s, short dark hair, Mediterranean look," she intones. "Sorry, dear. You fit the profile to a T."

Profile of a terrorist. Me? I'm momentarily appalled, but the feeling quickly gives way to another. It's good to know there is a system to the security.

Now I'm in Geneva, visiting friends and wandering around in rich people's yards, as free as a bird. It makes me feel uneasy.

Across the lake is the Rothschild mansion, nearby the expanse of the U.N. Headquarters. Geneva's famous jet of water is spraying a fine, tall mist. But I am too distressed and astonished by the lack of neighborhood security measures to truly take it all in.

I didn't think like this before.

I wish I didn't now.

Giving

She's a registered nurse, but she isn't employed just now. "It's difficult to get a job in Naples," she explains, "and also I have two small children." The shift work, the odd hours demanded of a full-time nurse, would leave too big a gap in her family life at a time when it's important to be at home.

So she volunteers with the Red Cross, she trains nursing assistants, she gives presentations on hygiene and dental care at the school and a local day-care center. She's learned to make adjustments in her life, as every military wife must do. "But I don't volunteer in a hospital," she says carefully. "I don't do nursing in my specialty for free. I feel I should be paid for that." The feeling is part of her professionalism, and because she is a professional it has notable exceptions. Like a certain Sunday when tragedy struck the Marine headquarters in Beirut.

She was sewing a child's Halloween costume when her husband told her the news. "The Marines in Beirut have been blown up," he said, and they turned on the radio to find out more. "The more I listened the more distressed and anxious I became," she recalls, "especially knowing the size of our medical facility here — it's small. There were recall notices on the air for all hospital personnel. But it's hard to get information here. How many people listen to the radio on a Sunday? And so many people don't have telephones."

After hearing the recall about three times she phoned the hospital. Did they need help? "Yes," a harried voice told her. "We have a blood drive on and we're in desperate need of people to come in and assist."

"I'm on my way," she answered. It was, she says now, a very automatic thing to do. "I wouldn't expect less from any RN."

When she got to the base hospital, fifteen miles from her home, the place was already jumping. "There was a heightened sense of response, adrenaline was flowing. The lobby was filling up with personnel in scrub suits, but there was nothing for them to do."

Word went out that the patients would be coming in soon. Forty-two injured Marines were expected to arrive in groups of twelve at two-hour intervals. She hadn't been at the hospital long when the air ambulance began to practice touch-and-go landings. "The sound of the propellers, the noise of the helicopter engine — it was a very emotional time," she says. "But it was all completely professional."

By now Marines from the nearby barracks were arriving to donate blood, and she was kept busy assisting with that work. Seeing these men, fit and healthy as they were, she couldn't help but think of the others who would be arriving soon. "I think the reason I went in," she says thoughtfully, "is that I took it personally. These Marines, they're just young boys. I really wanted to do something to help."

She is not, she points out, a "professional volunteer." But there are times when a person is needed and it's a duty — maybe almost an honor — to respond. "I don't think you get many chances in life to do something for people who've been in a warlike situation, who've been brutally attacked. You feel upset, angry, but you don't often have a chance to do something that contributes to the welfare of those people."

At the end of the day word came down that only twelve Marines would be brought to Naples, and ten of those were ambulatory. There was more than enough blood on hand, the normal staff could handle all the patients. There was nothing left for a volunteer to do.

So she went on home, feeling a little sick from giving blood and then not eating, feeling a little tired, a little cold. But underneath those feelings, in the mix of the shock of the tragedy and the fatigue from a good day's work, she felt something else as well. She couldn't help but feel a little proud for doing her best when it was most needed.

Memorial Day

It doesn't take a Memorial Day to make her think of them. She thinks of them whenever she comes across them, and since she's been living in Europe it seems like that happens a lot.

There's Luxembourg, of course. Everybody goes there. Just beyond the airport there are signs for the American Cemetery. General Patton is buried there, beneath a cross as simple as the rest. And there are thousands of crosses; they stretch whitely across the acres.

It's quite a sight. It's something that makes one think. Watching the tourists as they meander about she can see that nearly everyone is affected, nearly everyone pauses for at least an instant of serious reflection before returning to the tour bus.

Two kilometers down the road is another cemetery, but not so many visitors go there. "*Deutsches Friedof*" says an obscure sign. German cemetery. The color of the crosses is dark, no tablets bear heroic inscriptions. This cemetery seems to her too somber, too sad, almost apologetic. No one comes to tell these soldiers they did not die in vain.

She grew up in Arlington. Maybe that's why these places draw her. But in Arlington the cemetery is big and bold. There is more pride than sadness. It is a place of honor, but it has no sense of unity, no single story that touches. Arlington inspires awe, but it has never made her weep.

She's been to Gettysburg a dozen times, but that is a place of historical fascination, and Vicksburg seems the same. Those are the military cemeteries she knows in the U.S. Why they seem so different from the ones in Europe she cannot fully explain.

It was the ground at Verdun that awakened her to the full horrors of that place. Uneven ground, more like a choppy sea than the earth she thought she knew. Trees still grow at strange angles and everywhere she stepped there were depressions so she had to be careful not to twist an ankle. She mentioned the oddity out loud and was shocked by the explanation — a thousand mortar rounds a day for months on end will turn God's earth into something like you never saw before. She went to the cemetery there with a brutal image of how so many died.

At Omaha Beach the cliffs astounded her. Steep and rocky, scaled by Americans climbing to almost certain death. She entered the U.S. cemetery nearby with a special sense of respect.

But these are the places she's known about. Along with Bastogne and Anzio, they're part of the history she studied as a schoolgirl.

It's the other places that really bring it home. The little ones, the ones she didn't know about. A Scottish unit lies buried in Minturno, Italy, on the coastal road just north of Naples. Next to an ancient amphitheater, in two small acres of manicured grass, the tiny cemetery surprised her. Just what happened in the area she does not know, only that five or six hundred men died over a three-day period in the winter of 1944.

Another day and fifty miles away she saw a French flag fluttering in the breeze and stopped to find a battalion's resting place in the middle of the countryside near no town at all. *Mort pour la France* is the inscription on each cross. Died for France. No further details necessary.

At Monte Cassino she knew she would find such resting places. She passed them on her way to the restored abbey. It was the one at the top that stopped her — a Polish military cemetery in the heart of Italy. Poles, she marvelled, and wondered how they ever came to fight at this battle.

No, it doesn't take Memorial Day to remind her. She remembers them, something in her heart honors them, each time they meet.

So on Memorial Day she thinks of something else. She thinks of the living. And she wonders sadly: "If the horror should come again, will any among *them* be left to remember?"

Wall of Names

It is a bright and sunny spring day when I first see the Vietnam War Memorial in Washington, D.C. Tourists are strolling along the edges of a pleasant pool, the government buildings gleam impressively in the sun. Only a small, discreet sign points to the monument.

There are many visitors on this balmy Washington day. A father and his daughter pass me as I make my way along the rocky path. "Well," I hear him tell her as she looks a question, "we made a terrible mistake."

A small stand holds the list of names and directions on where to find each one. The people around it wait patiently, search carefully. "It was a big war for them," I hear one Asian-looking man tell another. "Quite a lot of people died."

At first I don't see the whole long wall. As I round the final bend I am looking down at the path—the stones are somewhat widely spaced here, and the heels of my shoes keep slipping down between them. I am afraid of ruining a good pair of shoes or twisting an ankle.

So it is as I look down at my feet, filled with concern for an impractical pair of shoes, that I see the first names. They are inches off the ground, for the wall is tiny at first, emerging almost innocently from the ground. But it grows and overwhelms, and as I walk its length its presence wipes out every other awareness. Now it is as tall as I, now taller, now so tall I could never reach its top. And every space upon this black wall is covered with a name, and every name a person who died in war.

I am thinking of a genteel luncheon in New York City a few days earlier. I had a civilized discussion with two ladies over salad. Ah yes, they told me, the military, very necessary. We support it. Most important. We pay our taxes gladly. But—and this is the clincher—after some such talk, one woman leaned forward and looked me in the eye and said, "Not my son." And her friend leaned toward me and stared fiercely and said, "Raise the taxes. Improve the GI Bill so others will go. But not my son. Never my son."

Now I am standing at this tall, black wall in Washington. It is covered with names, and everyone is someone's son, someone's daughter. How many times that cry must have been heard when the wire came, when the official car arrived. "Not my son! Never my son!"

There are flags and flowers and wreaths at this monument. The eighth-grade class of St. Joan of Arc School in Chagrin Falls, Ohio, has given an impressive wreath of red, white, and blue ribbons. In another place I see a simple white silk flower with a message attached: "I love you and miss you."

Standing by this wall, I feel such a terrible sense of loss. There is nothing wrong about this feeling and yet, when my vision blurs, I am embarrassed. And as I walk the length of this wall, from behind the safety of dark glasses I watch the faces of the other visitors. Certainly there is no gaiety among them, no smiles, no lack of decorum. But neither is there mourning.

There are people looking for specific names, people taking in the measure of this imposing edifice, people glad to be alive on a balmy day in Washington.

I am glad that I have seen this, but it leaves me with no sense of rightness. Here, the names of so many, many sons. Why, even for the space of this one brief visit, are mine the only tears?

10

All's Fair

*Stuff about Military Life That
Most Civilians Don't Know*

A Handy Guide to the Hierarchy

It's often hard for civilians, spouses, and a soldier's in-laws to understand the military hierarchy. Everybody usually knows something about the rank structure, but few family members can count rockers quick enough to know just who they're looking at.

For those who are still trying to figure out what's going on, here's a handy guide to what some of those titles really mean:

General. This is the big man on base. His duties include touring the facilities, conferring behind closed doors, and ducking in and out of cocktail parties. Making extemporaneous remarks is the general's real forte, as he is expected to address everything but the invitations to his next soirée.

The general is a nice guy, but his immediate subordinates are terrors. They initiate and carry out all the nasty decisions. The general doesn't usually find out about these bad doings until it's too late, so the soldiers are always on his side.

Colonel. The colonel is not as important as the general, although so far no one has dared to tell him this. He is sometimes called in to make speeches when the general is unavailable, and he has been known to practice his material on random groups, such as three people waiting for the traffic light to change.

The colonel is normally in charge of a special task force that is studying an important issue, such as the practicality of re-inking typewriter ribbons in the field. He is not at liberty to discuss his current work, but if you ask him about his days as a platoon leader he will almost certainly buy you a drink.

CO. The commanding officer is the person who is directly in charge. His rank is immaterial—when a soldier speaks of the CO he refers to the person he fears and admires most in all the world. The CO may sometimes mention the wishes of the General or Colonel, but soldiers recognize this for the empty power ploy it is. They know that it is their CO who causes them to be inspected for possible violation of the world's most meaningless requirements, who can add horrible definition to the phrase "extra duties as assigned," and who holds the power to confer that glorious state of euphoria known as a "training holiday."

First Sergeant. The CO makes broad decisions and the First Sergeant makes them happen. Unlike the Sergeant Major, whose attention is focused on the quality of the service at the NCO Club, and the Master Sergeant, whose function has never been defined, the First Sergeant carries out a meaningful job. It is he who ensures that soldiers' TA-50, barracks rooms, and personal lives are all in good order. Although many have tried, it is virtually impossible to deceive this man. The nightly prayers of many a soldier contain a note of hope that the First Sergeant will keep that which he knows to himself.

Corporal. Corporals got a big name by doing heroic acts in World War II movies. In reality, most corporals are just soldiers who haven't yet made sergeant, but like to act as if they have. Corporals on the whole are not a bad lot, but neither are they quite so nifty as so many of them mistakenly believe.

Soldiers. Everybody who's in the Army is a soldier, of course, but the real troops are those in grades E-nothing to PFC. These are sincere, dedicated personnel, who labor for the sheer sense of accomplishment.

Nine times out of ten your basic soldier could give the First

Sergeant quite a few pointers, but generally he prefers not to embarrass the NCO.

Above all, soldiers have the most accurate perspective of the military hierarchy. They realize that they are on the bottom with nowhere to go but up. Luckily, this penetratingly realistic view of the Army structure makes them ideal candidates for advancement.

Call It Otis

To be frank, I am not much for New Year's resolutions. In my experience they're just another means of brutally demonstrating how weak-willed I really am. How many days will it take me to fall off the diet? Not many. How many times will I actually do the new exercise program? Too few. How hard will I work to improve my syntax? Let's not discuss it.

Instead of making silly personal resolutions for '86, I'd like to propose a military resolution. The resolution is: Let's not name weapons after people anymore.

I've been thinking about this ever since the Sgt. York debacle. It used to be that when I thought of Sgt. York, I thought of courage, heroism, and derring-do. Now, when I think of Sgt. York, I think of duds. Mention Sgt. York and a sound pops into my mind. The sound is phhhhhhht.

It may not be fair, but I can't help it.

A lot of important military figures have had weapons named after them. It's especially popular to name tanks after generals. I don't understand this. Is it because they keep charging no matter what?

Whatever the reason, it probably isn't a very good one. If you could ask them, I'll bet Sherman, Walker, Patton, and Abrams would all tell you they'd rather have something else named after them. Something more stable and permanent, like a place.

I've always thought Clay Caserne in Berlin was an impressive-sounding name. I also liked the ring of Cambrai-Fritsch Caserne in Darmstadt, even if it is named after two people at once. And I found living on Gorgas Road at Schofield Barracks in Hawaii very satisfactory, though I often wondered who Gorgas was and what he did to have such a short road named for him.

Clay, Cambrai, Fritsch, and Gorgas are all good names for places, but lousy names for weapons. MX is a good weapon name because it sounds futuristic and dangerous. Of course that's just the temporary name. What if it ultimately gets named after a general named, say, Otis? How threatened will our enemies really feel if they hear that Otis is coming?

Weapons should have names like Trident, Chaparral, and Warthog. These are good, strong, nearly invincible names. And they don't mess up our memories of some decent individual who deserves to be remembered.

Of course the Navy has its own protocol of how to name ships. Personally, I prefer the stately names, like *Utah* and *Iowa*. I'm a little upset about the *Coral Sea*. Why do we have a ship with that name? Shouldn't it be named after some American place? Our ships should be named after national bodies of water, like the East River or Crater Lake or the Erie Canal.

Then there's the *Nimitz*. It's an aircraft carrier, which really makes it a weapon. I don't think it should be named after a person. Name the port after the good admiral. Then name the ship something more appropriate. Name it *Idaho* or *Vulcan Fire*. Something inspiring like that.

I suppose there are some people who may have a spiritual problem with naming weapons after Olympian gods. I can relate to that. Not to mention the fact that the Olympians are getting close to all used up. Pretty soon we'll be naming bazooka guns after Cupid.

But not to worry. There are plenty of other sources of names for weapons. Why not name a few after the seven dwarfs? You know — Happy, Grumpy, Dopey, and like that. I can think of several weapons those would be good names for.

One thing I don't know is, who decides how to name weapons? Certainly no one has ever asked me for my ideas on the subject. Maybe there's a bureau, like for hurricanes.

If there is such a bureau, and you're on it, and right now you're thinking of naming a glorious new weapon after a revered military hero, please do us all a favor.

Think about Sgt. York, and then . . . think again.

Equal Ashtrays for All

I've about had it with the ridiculous items the Navy and Air Force are continually buying themselves. Recently it was disclosed that the Navy was billed $660 for an ashtray and $400 for a socket wrench. You'll recall the Air Force was presented tabs of $495 for a hammer and around $700 for a toilet seat. It's incredible. It's outrageous. Why hasn't the Army been getting any of this stuff?

Maybe I've missed the news, but every one of these incidents seems to deal with Navy and Air Force acquisitions. Oh sure, the whistle-blowers are trying to focus attention on alleged waste, but they are missing the point. The way the picture adds up to me, the Army has been getting shortchanged.

Now, I don't want to get into an interservice rivalry. I realize we're all in the military together and it's a mistake to point out the superiority of one service over another. I know it's best to put on a humble front so other folks won't feel bad. Let's face it, overweight people have to be somewhere too, and I think the Navy is as good a place as any. When it comes to the Air Force, why it's only natural that it would be made up of space cadets.

But those are not significant points. I, for one, have never been interested in making an issue of them. Sure, some people like to bob around in boats, some people like to hang out in the sky, and others want their feet right on this wonderful Earth the way the good Lord intended. I'd be the last one to make any judgments over certain people's preferences just because I happen to think they're wacko. It wouldn't be right.

But this most recent business of the high-priced parts has me really aggravated. I don't want to say it's a conspiracy, but I'm hard-pressed to avoid concluding there's skulduggery afoot.

Most people are looking at the thing all backward. They're thinking the Navy and Air Force are going to get egg on their faces because they paid hundreds of dollars for a simple tool. Well, they're not thinking right.

What we actually have here is a classic public relations ploy. It goes like this: The Navy blows the whistle on itself for the $660 ashtray. Big publicity. Navy officials apologize. They berate the contractor. They demand a refund. They convince the public that they really are cutting back on wasteful expenditures. In the end they get to keep a really neat ashtray that's actually worth $660.

Devious, huh?

The Air Force has plainly been doing the same thing. If it's in cahoots with the Navy, I cannot say. But it's gotten so that every time I see a plane, I imagine the pilot sitting on his $700 toilet seat laughing at us Army types.

What we have to do is figure out a way to fight back. It has to be something significant. We can't reveal we've been paying $3.98 for MREs that are only worth $2.75. You don't get any publicity out of a confession like that.

I've got a better idea. The Army should order 100,000 silk umbrellas hand-painted in a camouflage design. I've seen some nice ones in a little shop near the Ponte Vecchio in Florence, Italy. The design wasn't exactly classic camouflage, but that's a detail.

These probably will run us about $70 each, but we'll ask the vendor to charge us $500 each. He's a nice man, and I'm sure he'd be glad to help out. That puts our bill to him at $50 million, about the same as we'd pay for a couple of Abrams tanks, right?

Next, we leak the deal. The newspapers headline the story, and the Army gets to point out it's going to be incredibly vigilant in two areas from now on, because, not only are the umbrellas outrageously overpriced, but soldiers are not allowed to carry them anyway.

Oh, yeah, there's another bennie as well. With the money we save on the umbrellas, we get to buy the tanks.

Military Soap

Some military folks are still wondering why the American public sometimes rebels against defense spending. They don't realize the public can never really appreciate the military until they get to know it better. And the best way to get to know an institution that actually encompasses an entire lifestyle, as the Army does, is for TV to broadcast a daily soap opera about it.

So I've decided to send a treatment for a pilot around to a few top producers. It goes like this:

"The Officers" (working title) is envisioned as an ongoing afternoon program that will reveal the difficult challenges faced by today's Army personnel, their spouses and families. Not just a superficial examination of boring official matters, "The Officers" will reveal that military personnel live sexy, exciting lives, just like doctors, oilmen, and politicians. The primary characters are . . .

Capt. Wotley. Philip Wotley is a company commander who aspires to the highest levels of achievement. He will let nothing stand in his way. Wotley is divorced. He tells people his wife, Mina, left him for another man, but this is just a ploy to elicit sympathy. In fact, she sought a divorce when Wotley insisted she work at least 30 hours a week in the thrift shop and hold a monthly tea at her home in an effort to impress the general's wife.

The sole chink in Wotley's evil armor is his lust for Coquette Ferd.

Lt. Col. Joshua Ferd. Ferd, a member of the general's staff, is a conniving schemer who longs to be made post commander so he can live in the big house by the gate. Ferd and his wife successfully carried out a diabolical plan to cause many of his competitors to gain excessive weight by frequently inviting them over for dessert parties. No one ever declines because men love to be around . . .

Coquette Ferd. Coquette has cooperated in several of her husband's unethical efforts to get ahead, but her heart was not in it. Coquette considers her great and alluring beauty to be a handicap in life and longs to be appreciated for her mind. Coquette is a nuclear physicist who gave up her career to marry Ferd. But she is sad, because since entering military life she has had no one to talk to, except . . .

Maj. Gen. Will Goode. Goode is a fine man, proof that the best do rise to the top. Goode strives to see that the soldiers are all treated fairly, that the quality of training is tops, and that the Officer's Club serves decent lunches. Goode admires Coquette Ferd in a fatherly way and enjoys discussing nuclear techtronics with her. Unfortunately, this relationship has been misinterpreted by . . .

Gertrude Goode. Gertrude, Maj. Gen. Goode's wife, is insanely jealous of Coquette Ferd. Gertrude feels she may be losing the general's attentions and has secretly started attending a series of Jane Fonda Workout Classes. But she is well aware of the danger of her enterprise — the general would be furious if he knew. He hates Jane Fonda.

More important, the general has been nominated for a sensitive assignment, and Gertrude believes the job opportunity will be lost if a secret from Goode's past is exploited by Wotley or Ferd.

PFC Knix. Knix is a clerk in the general's outer outer office. He does not know that he is actually the general's son as a result of a mistake the general made while working late one night early in his career. Knix is a fine young man, but he hates all officers, because he thinks they are evil and conniving. He has rejected the general's friendly overtures. But Knix does not dislike the wives. When he is not on duty, he lusts after Coquette Ferd, because she is gorgeous. He lusts after Gertrude Goode, who seems to be getting more shapely all the time. And he lusts after Mina Wotley.

First episode synopsis:

PFC Knix learns his real mother is a paratrooper who deserted his father because he was a "leg." Knix is getting dangerously close to the truth.

Coquette's fattening dinner party is ruined when, in a fit of conscience, she deliberately lets the cream sauce curdle. Nobody gains any weight. Ferd's promotion is not assured.

Wotley spots Gertrude doing her Fonda routine and threatens to tell all unless she agrees to forge her husband's signature on an OER that states that Wotley walks on water.

Mina Wotley falls for Ferd and says she'll do "anything" for him. Together they hatch a plot to discredit Philip by bleaching his BDUs the day before a big parade.

Maj. Gen. Goode stays in his office and is happy. He doesn't know what's happening.

Dare to Be Bare

I've just had an extraordinarily interesting letter from a friend of mine. Her husband has finally made good in the business world, they have all the money they could want, and they've just taken a luxury vacation of the type of which they've always dreamed. What they did was, they went to an island in the Caribbean and stayed naked for a week.

Now you might think this would be a thrifty kind of vacation, but it wasn't. In fact, it was quite expensive. It's not as if they just went off to some beach and peeled off their swimsuits. They went to an exclusive resort for rich people who are beyond caring about crass material things like clothes. After all, naked is not something you want to be with just any Joe off the street. You need to be with the right people.

My friend's ruminations on this vacation experience were revealing. She confided that emotions are very evident when fundamentals are disclosed. Many of the other wives, she felt, were envious of her trim form. Quite a few of the men were clearly admiring, no matter how subtle they tried to be. But the naked people all joined together in mocking the ridiculous tourists who occasionally wandered through the nude territory in their silly bathing suits.

The bottom line, my friend reports, is that there was a unique harmony among those nude, brought about, she's convinced, by the absence of gross outer trappings.

Now there's a thought.

It put me in mind of all the meetings and briefings I've attended and how the outer trappings distract everybody and often affect the gathering's outcome even more than the information being presented. Too many people spend more time staring at the Colonel's eagles than listening to his remarks. I'll bet things would hum along a lot more efficiently if everybody were nude.

Of course, I'm not thinking that lower-level humdrum meetings should be conducted in the buff. I'm thinking only of the most important, critically significant meetings. The idea would be to start with a precedent-setting meeting to get the ball rolling on this idea. Say, the next U.S.–Soviet Summit.

The Russians are an earthy kind of people, and I'm willing to bet Gorbachev would see the many potential advantages.

I don't doubt the Soviet leader would immediately recognize the economic advantages of being naked in the U.S. He'd save a lot on Western-tailored suits. But the key thing would be the effect on the meeting itself. It would do the world a lot of good if our leaders could see once and for all how insignificant their actual differences are.

Also, it's hard to be pompous and uncompromising when you're in the nude. My friends' experience reveals plainly that naked people have trouble concealing their motivations. They're therefore more likely to be friendly and to seek common ground. Who can be sly when all his dimples are showing? A nude world summit would be certain to result in significant agreements in a short time — especially if the meeting room were slightly underheated.

Such a policy would work equally well at the highest military meetings. Under the present system, it's too hard for generals to concentrate. They are too confused by so many stars flashing from so many shoulderboards, as they do when the Joint Chiefs get together. Eliminate those shoulderboards, along with other outer gear, and they'll have nothing to think about but the subject at hand.

Given this policy, the Chiefs will quite rightly refuse to attend meetings that have the primary purpose of strutting fancy uniforms, since no one will be wearing any uniforms at all. They'll confine themselves, at last, to matters of actual significance. More of them will stay awake during briefings when the briefings are held debriefed.

I'm convinced the rituals and outer accoutrements that accompany policy-making gatherings all too often completely inhibit their effectiveness. My friend swears by the philosophy that getting back to basic assets results in a more humanistic view of all life's situations. I think there's a good chance she's right, so why not try out her concept on a broader scale?

Traditionalists will resist, I know, but without change there is no progress. You're never going to get anywhere if you don't try something nude once in a while.

Mailish Myths

I've just read about a new study which claims the average man has a thought about sex once every 15 seconds, while women think about sex only once each minute. Silly me. I had the impression those periodic glazed looks meant my friends were overly preoccupied with the progression of the talks in Geneva.

Who these sex-crazed average people are I cannot imagine, but you may rest assured I am not among them. There's no way I have time to think a sexy thought once every 60 seconds. My mind is too tied up with thinking about the mail.

You probably think the mail is a boring thing to focus on, but it isn't. It's fascinating. My fantasies concerning the mail make the Cosmo Girl's desert island daydreams look like the doldrums indeed.

These mental meanderings are my favorite way to pass time that might otherwise be wasted. While waiting in bank lines, for instance, instead of doing invisible isometric buttock stretches, I let my mind run rampant with mailish myths of my own invention.

While I jog each morning, my thoughts naturally drift to potential postal arrivals and the good news they may bring.

Even while engaged in such mundane activities as mashing potatoes, sitting poolside, or sipping cocktails, my attention often slips off to a magical place of castles in the air where letters reach their addressees in 24 hours and postage is never due.

It would be boring if my only thoughts had to do with the question of the mail's arrival. I've long passed that point, however, and drifted on to more sophisticated points of imagination.

I think, for instance, about the box of towels my father mailed me some two months ago. Where are they now, and what is happening to them?

Perhaps they are in the creaky bottom of a ship's hold, tossed and jostled among the crates of Kuwait-bound cases of Perrier water, with which they were mistakenly loaded.

Perhaps they lie among a jumble of boxes stacked upon the tarmac at some impersonally large international airport, patiently waiting for space that is available, soaking up the gentle rain.

Or maybe my towels already are doing other duty. Maybe the carefully wrapped box burst under the pressure of travel and my towels progressed on to a new life as packing material. Or maybe the address smeared and the package was sent on to an unintended recipient, a soldier's wife with name and address just a digit or two off from mine, who even now is telling her husband, "I never ordered these towels. They're too expensive!"

I know the towels may yet arrive, or else they may not. Worrying about that detail is only futile frustration. More interesting to me would be the saga of their journey, if only it could be revealed.

Sometimes the letters that float in, haggard and worn, bear tantalizing clues. "Left at JFK in container presumed empty" is one of the more interesting stamps the APO uses. The words conjure up images of a huge metal bin, heartlessly vacant with the exception of my one small letter wedged into a back corner, unnoticed just long enough to allow its contents to become uselessly dated.

Sometimes the late letter arrives marked with the APO to which it was mistakenly sent. 09Q21Z. I know that place! It's a small town in Germany, not much there, a rather dismal assignment altogether. Perhaps my unexpected letter gave those people a moment's comfort.

There's no doubt about it, I'm happy to leave sexy thinking to others. I haven't time for such. The mail comes once a day, five days a week. Do I think about it every minute? At least.

One little fantasy that sometimes pops up concerns a trip to the post office. I walk in and simultaneously realize that (a) they are out of 22-cent stamps, and (b) the new mail clerk is Warren Beatty. He asks if he can help me, but I don't answer. For an instant, all my attention is on a thought that has jumped into my head from nowhere. It has nothing to do with the mail.

Year of Values

This is a somewhat melancholy time of year. On the one hand, we're heading into a delightful celebratory holiday season. On the other hand, the Year of Values is almost over.

I'm saddened by this because the Year of Values seems to have completely passed me by. I've been invited to no special parties, received no colorful mailings, gotten no extra support in my constant effort to keep my own values on the highest level. I know the Year of Values has been happening out there, but I haven't been a part of it. I feel left out.

And it's not as if it's the first time, either.

The Year of Values is just one of several special years the Army has put on. They started in 1981 with "Yorktown — The Spirit of Victory." Frankly, it's my view that they got off on the wrong foot. Yorktown was a big winner, but let's look at the facts. The British had 6,000 soldiers. The Americans and the French teamed up together and had about 17,000 men. If it were me picking the Years, I'd pick another battle to memorialize.

In 1982 we had the Year of Fitness, which was a big improvement. It's hard to appreciate the Spirit of Victory when you're not officially out fighting anybody. But we all care about fitness. The Year of Fitness was a year with a point—you got fit or you got out.

Next came the Year of Excellence, which was not, in fact, all that great. And the Year of the Family, in 1984, had a lot of possibilities, only some of which worked out. 1985 was the Year of Leadership. And this, the year that is almost over, is the Year of Values.

There's a lot to be said for not having theme years. The Navy and the Air Force seem to get along just fine without them, although they occasionally pick up on the ideas on a smaller scale.

I know at least one Air Force Base had a "Month of the Family" in 1984, and the Navy base where I lived put on a very nice "Spouse Day." You'd think a whole Year of the Family would be a better deal than a mere Spouse Day. I'm not so sure. Some people got plaques on Spouse Day and received unsolicited praise. The Year of the Family didn't include prizes.

Part of the problem here is a matter of public relations. I happen to know a film was made to celebrate the Year of Values. I haven't seen the film, but I wish I'd had the chance. It's been my experience that Army films are the greatest.

Not too long ago I saw a masterpiece called *Wings and Talons*, which is all about the 101st Airborne (Air Assault) Division. I loved that film. I loved seeing the helicopters show off their maneuverability. I loved the announcer's deep voice and the way he described the many advantages of air assault. In short, *Wings and Talons* made a believer out of me. For days afterward, if anyone happened to ask me to name my favorite thing, I'd immediately say, "Air assault!" Normally my favorite thing is air defense.

That's why I think if I'd seen the movie about the Year of Values I might appreciate the concept a little more.

It's too late for that now. The Year of Values soon ends, the film will go into some dark archives, and the Army will move on to other things.

What I'd like to see them move on to would be a different kind of theme year. A Year with real meaning. Like maybe a Year of No Uniform Changes. Or possibly a Year Free of Field Duty. Or even something practical, like a Year of Maintenance, or a Year of Long Leaves.

Best of all would be a Year of Awards. That would be a Year in which no one gets an award unless they've actually done something to deserve it, but at the end of the Year, everyone who can still remember the theme gets an oak leaf sprig.

Guidance

Sometimes we have a tendency to moan about the advantages civilian life offers, like the chance to make a million overnight by becoming a rock star or inventing a wrinkle cream that works. But no matter how you look at it, it's undeniably true military life has a lot of pluses that are totally missing from the civilian world.

The thing that leaps to mind, of course, is Guidance. Guidance, so far as I can tell, exists only in military life. Ask a civilian about Guidance and he's likely to tell you guidance is what sends missiles in the right direction. Which just goes to show how little he knows, because that's not Guidance at all.

Guidance is the thing you will do, not only because it's been determined that it's the best thing for you to do, but because if you don't do it your whole entire little world will come crashing down around you. Painfully.

In the old days, before the military hierarchy had evolved into its present caring mode, there were only Orders. Like when the First Sergeant would say, "Everybody gets a haircut this afternoon whether they need it or not! And that's an Order!" Or sometimes word might go out at staff call, "All quarters lawns are to be spruce at 10 A.M. tomorrow when a VIP group tours post. General's Orders."

We still have orders, of course. A lot of times they're written out, and they tell you where you'll be going next time you move. Sometimes they're delivered orally, and they tell you you will spend your morning picking up any candy wrappers that have drifted onto the quad.

Guidance is different. It is more gentle, more humane. It comes to you in a user-friendly way. Guidance is when an NCO tells his troops, "The leaves on the plants in the Headquarters Building are getting dusty. Our Guidance says they should be clean and shiny." That's when you know you'll be spending your morning polishing philodendrons.

Some people don't understand about Guidance. It comes to them in such an understated way, they think following Guidance is optional. It isn't. What happens to you when you don't follow Guidance is the same thing that happens when you don't follow orders. You find yourself in deep kimchee.

Those who don't catch on to the importance of following Guidance probably don't realize where it's coming from. Guidance comes from generals, and usually only one general at any given post issues bona fide Guidance. That will be the general who is the most important commander. That way, when junior people start running around saying, "The General's Guidance on this is . . ." there's no confusion about just which general is involved.

The fact is, one hardly ever hears the term *Guidance* unless it is appended to the word *General*. There are probably a few crotchety colonels and upstart majors who attempt to issue Guidance, but it is not valid. Those lower-ranking officers may issue orders, but they simply don't have the clout to give out Guidance.

How does Guidance get started? Few people really know. Most likely it's issued in an informal way. Like when the V Corps Commander tells his secretary, "I really like *Volksmarching*. I wish everyone would try it." The next thing you know, it's being announced at staff call that "the General's Guidance is that we should all participate in *Volksmarches* this month. Here are the sign-up sheets."

Unlike Orders, Guidance often applies to family members. "I hate to see women wearing those ugly sweatsuits," the General might tell an aide. Next thing you know, the Guidance is out: No more unattractive athletic clothes to be worn in the PX.

The good thing about Guidance is you can be sure it comes from someone who knows the way. The bad thing is we don't always know just where he's taking us.

But that's okay. Guidance—the General's Guidance—is always there, leading us to do the right thing in all manner of situations. I guess I have to admit there's little doubt about its importance.

Without Guidance, we'd be lost.